PUBLISHING

D0544875

Kaplan Publishing are constantly finding new ways to make a difference to your studies and our exciting online resources really do offer something different to AAT students looking for exam success.

FOR THE FIRST TIME, KAPLAN'S AAT TEXTS COME WITH FREE EN-gage ONLINE RESOURCES SO THAT YOU CAN STUDY ANYTIME, ANYWHERE

Having purchased this Kaplan Text, you have access to the following online study materials:

- An online version of the Text
- Fixed Online Tests with instant answers

How to access your online resources

- **Kaplan Financial students** will already have a Kaplan EN-gage account and these extra resources will be available to you online. You do not need to register again, as this process was completed when you enrolled. If you are having problems accessing online materials, please ask your course administrator.
- **If you purchased through Kaplan Flexible Learning or via the Kaplan Publishing website** you will automatically receive an e-mail invitation to Kaplan EN-gage online. Please register your details using this e-mail to gain access to your content. If you do not receive the e-mail or book content, please contact Kaplan Flexible Learning.
- **If you are already a registered Kaplan EN-gage user** go to www.EN-gage.co.uk and log in. Select the 'add a book' feature and enter the ISBN number of this book and the unique pass key at the bottom of this card. Then click 'finished' or 'add another book'. You may add as many books as you have purchased from this screen.
- **If you are a new Kaplan EN-gage user** register at www.EN-gage.co.uk and click on the link contained in the e-mail we sent you to activate your account. Then select the 'add a book' feature, enter the ISBN number of this book and the unique pass key at the bottom of this card. Then click 'finished' or 'add another book'.

Your Code and Information

This code can only be used once for the registration of one book online. This registration will expire when the final sittings for the examinations covered by this book have taken place. Please allow one hour from the time you submitted your book details for us to process your request.

Iocb-KkGU-7vVe-t1ry

Please be aware that this code is case-sensitive and you will need to include the dashes within the passcode, but not when entering the ISBN. For further technical support, please visit www.EN-gage.co.uk

SPREADSHEET SOFTWARE

Qualifications and Credit Framework

Level 3 Diploma in Accounting

SPREADSHEET SOFTWARE

British Library Cataloguing-in-Publication Data

A catalogue record for this book is available from the British Library.

Published by
Kaplan Publishing UK
Unit 2, The Business Centre
Molly Millars Lane
Wokingham
Berkshire
RG41 2QZ

ISBN 978-0-85732-219-7

The text in this material and any others made available by any Kaplan Group company does not amount to advice on a particular matter and should not be taken as such. No reliance should be placed on the content as the basis for any investment or other decision or in connection with any advice given to third parties. Please consult your appropriate professional adviser as necessary. Kaplan Publishing Limited and all other Kaplan group companies expressly disclaim all liability to any person in respect of any losses or other claims, whether direct, indirect, incidental, consequential or otherwise arising in relation to the use of such materials.

Printed in Great Britain by WM Print Ltd, Walsall.

We are grateful to the Association of Accounting Technicians for permission to reproduce past assessment materials and example tasks based on the new syllabus. The solutions to past answers and similar activities in the style of the new syllabus have been prepared by Kaplan Publishing.

We are grateful to HM Revenue and Customs for the provision of tax forms, which are Crown Copyright and are reproduced here with kind permission from the Office of Public Sector Information.

CONTENTS

INTRODUCTION

HOW TO USE THESE MATERIALS

These Kaplan Publishing learning materials have been carefully designed to make your learning experience as easy as possible and to give you the best chance of success in your AAT assessments.

They contain a number of features to help you in the study process.

The sections on the Unit Guide, the Assessment and Study Skills should be read before you commence your studies.

They are designed to familiarise you with the nature and content of the assessment and to give you tips on how best to approach your studies.

WORKBOOK

This workbook has been specially prepared for the revised AAT qualification introduced in July 2010. It uses a slightly different format to other Kaplan study texts at this level due to the nature of the syllabus content.

The screen shots for this text are based around Excel 2003. However, at the end of each section there is a 'pathway' box which shows you how to navigate to the required function in both Excel 2000 and Excel 2007.

There are also 'tips and shortcuts' that will highlight quick ways in Excel to navigate to the correct function.

Throughout the workbook, there will be opportunities to test your knowledge through the activities. For some of these activities you will need to access pre-populated spreadsheets that you can view inside your Kaplan En-gage account. The login details for this account can be found on the insert contained within the workbook.

This workbook is predominantly designed as a study aid used within the classroom or as a distance learning student aid.

Please note that suggested answers to all the activities you encounter in the workbook can be accessed through your Kaplan EN-gage account.

UNIT GUIDE

Spreadsheet Software

6 credits

Purpose of the units

The AAT has stated that this unit describes the skills and competencies of an intermediate spreadsheet user.

Learning outcomes

On completion of these units the learner will be able to:

- Use a spreadsheet to enter, edit and organise numerical and other data

- Select and use appropriate formulas and data analysis tools and techniques to meet requirements

- Use tools and techniques to present, format and publish spreadsheet information

Knowledge

To perform this unit effectively you will need to know and understand the following:

		Chapter
1	**Use a spreadsheet to enter, edit and organise numerical and other data**	
1.1	Identify what numerical and other information is needed in the spreadsheet and how it should be structured	1,14
1.2	Enter numerical and other data accurately	2
1.3	Combine and link data from different sources	6,10
1.4	Store and retrieve spreadsheet files effectively, in line with local guidelines and conventions where applicable	1, 15, 17, 17
2	**Select and use appropriate formulas and data analysis tools and techniques to meet requirements**	
2.1	Explain what methods can be used to summarise, analyse and interpret spreadsheet data when to use them	9
2.2	Select and use a wide range of appropriate functions and formulas to meet calculation requirements	4, 6, 11
2.3	Select and use a range of tools and techniques to analyse and interpret data to meet requirements	18, 20, 22
2.4	Select and use forecasting tools and techniques	21
3	**Understand the current taxation principles of property income for an individual**	
3.1	Explain how to present and format spreadsheet information effectively to meet needs	3, 7
3.2	Select and use appropriate tools and techniques to format cells, rows, columns and worksheets effectively	3, 7, 8
3.3	Select and use appropriate tools and techniques to generate, develop and format charts and graphs	13, 19
3.4	Select and use appropriate page layout to present, print and publish spreadsheet information	5

KAPLAN PUBLISHING

Delivery guidance

The AAT have provided delivery guidance giving further details of the way in which the unit will be assessed.

The learner must be able to use existing spreadsheets, use spreadsheet templates, and also produce individual spreadsheets to meet certain requirements. They will need to identify what data (numerical and text) should be included within the spreadsheet and how the spreadsheet could be structured. There should be a planned structure to the spreadsheet and the design and layout should be appropriate to the task.

The learner must be able to enter and edit data accurately. They must be able to insert data into single and multiple cells, clear cells, edit cells, replicate data, copy, paste, find and replace, delete rows and columns and use absolute and relative cell references and add data and text to a chart. They should also be able to hide and protect cells and link data.

Learners must be able to store and retrieve spreadsheets. They could be assessed on using folders and files and should be able to use version control, import/export files into other documents and also archive information (back-up).

Learners must be able to use a wide range of formulae and function to complete calculations, and be able to use the design of formulas to meet calculation requirements. These could include mathematical, statistical, financial, conditional, look-up and logical functions.

Learners must be able to use a range of techniques to summarise data and then analyse and interpret the results. This could include the following summarising tools; Totals, sub-totals, sorting, filter rows and columns, tables, graphs, pivot tables and charts. The learner can be assessed on their judgement of when and how to use these methods.

Learners can be assessed on using tools, formulas and functions (for example data validation and pivot tables) needed to analyse the information within a spreadsheet. They must also be able to perform what-if scenarios, goal seek and data tables.

The learner must be able to produce presentable spreadsheets suitable for sharing with others (e.g. height, width, font, colour, shading, borders). The learner could be assessed on choosing the most appropriate way to display information. They must be correctly labelled. All chart types could be assessed such as bar, pie, bubble, doughnut, line and scatter graphs and pivot table reports. They must also be able to change chart type,

KAPLAN PUBLISHING

move, resize and annotate. Learners will also need to use the appropriate page set-up, margins, header and footer, page breaks, numbering and a date/time stamp.

Learners will need to check for errors in the accuracy of the numbers, the text, the results, the formulas, the layout and the relevance and accuracy of the analysis and interpretation. Once identified, learners must be able to rectify these errors and use the help facility, the audit formulas, and correct errors in circular references, calculations and results. They should also be able to validate data and remove invalid data.

Macros will not be assessed.

Examples

The AAT has also provided examples as to what could be assessed within each learning outcome. Please note this list is not exhaustive.

1 **Use a spreadsheet to enter, edit and organise numerical and other data**

1.1 The learner will be familiar with the component parts of a spreadsheet including; workbook, worksheet, column, row, cell, active cell, tab, page and panes/windows.

1.2 The learner will be able to use the following functions in editing and entering data across single or multiple cells; insert, delete, input/amend text and numerical data, copy, cut, paste, paste special, clear and find and replace.

1.3 The learner will be able to reorganise data in different formats and link, embed, and import/export data from a different source.

1.4 The learner will be able to use the following functions: Save, Save as, file name/rename, password protect files, back-up, and archive information.

2 **Select and use appropriate formulas and data analysis tools and techniques to meet requirements**

2.1 The learner will be to use the following functions in analysing and interpreting data: addition, subtraction, multiplication, division, sum, percentages, parentheses, pivot table, consolidation, sort data, filter data, data restriction, data validation, find and replace, look up, if, and, auto sum, relative references, absolute references and date.

2.2 The learner will be able to lock and hide cells.

2.3 The learner will be able to use the analysis tools within the spreadsheet. This can include, but not be restricted to, rank, percentile, moving averages and histograms.

2.4 The learner will be able to forecast using trend lines within the spreadsheet.

3   Use tools and techniques to present, format and publish spreadsheet information

3.1   Learners will be to use the following formatting tools: fixed decimal, 1000 separator, "£", formatting percentages, applying the accounting double underline to cells, text alignment, font and font size, cell justification, border and shading, merge cells, conditional formatting, page setup (margins, orientation, print area) and be able to print formula.

3.2   Learners will be able to insert and delete columns, rows, cells and to change the row height, column width

3.3   Learners will be able to hide and unhide cells and protect spreadsheets/cells

3.4   Learners will be able to produce and label charts and graphs (bar, line, pie, scatter, doughnut, bubble)

3.5   Learners will know how to use page layouts to present data and scale information for printing purposes.

3.6   learners will check spreadsheets for errors in content and in formula using the following functions: error checking, trace error and circular references and formula editing.

3.7   Learners will ensure that the information contained within the spreadsheet meets the needs of the recipient.

KAPLAN PUBLISHING

THE ASSESSMENT

The format of the assessment

Learners will normally be assessed by computer based assessment (CBA). Initially this assessment will be assessed by the centre that you are studying with. Therefore, it will not be an instant result received on the day you take the test. The AAT hope to introduce instant result feedback sometime in 2011.

Time allowed

The time allowed for this assessment is **90 mins.**

STUDY SKILLS

Preparing to study

Devise a study plan

Determine which times of the week you will study.

Split these times into sessions of at least one hour for study of new material. Any shorter periods could be used for revision or practice.

Put the times you plan to study onto a study plan for the weeks from now until the assessment and set yourself targets for each period of study – in your sessions make sure you cover the whole course, activities and the associated questions.

If you are studying more than one unit at a time, try to vary your subjects as this can help to keep you interested and see subjects as part of wider knowledge.

When working through your course, compare your progress with your plan and, if necessary, re-plan your work (perhaps including extra sessions) or, if you are ahead, do some extra revision / practice questions.

Effective studying

Active reading

You are not expected to learn the text by rote, rather, you must understand what you are reading and be able to use it to pass the assessment and develop good practice.

A good technique is to use SQ3Rs – Survey, Question, Read, Recall, Review:

1   **Survey the chapter**

    Look at the headings and read the introduction, and content, so as to get an overview of what the chapter deals with.

2   **Question**

    Whilst undertaking the survey ask yourself the questions you hope the chapter will answer for you.

3 Read

Read through the chapter thoroughly working through the activities and, at the end, making sure that you can meet the learning objectives highlighted on the first page.

4 Recall

At the end of each section and at the end of the chapter, try to recall the main ideas of the section / chapter without referring to the text. This is best done after short break of a couple of minutes after the reading stage.

5 Review

Check that your recall notes are correct.

You may also find it helpful to re-read the chapter to try and see the topic(s) it deals with as a whole.

Note taking

Taking notes is a useful way of learning, but do not simply copy out the text.

The notes must:

- be in your own words
- be concise
- cover the key points
- well organised
- be modified as you study further chapters in this text or in related ones.

Trying to summarise a chapter without referring to the text can be a useful way of determining which areas you know and which you don't.

Three ways of taking notes

1 Summarise the key points of a chapter

2 Make linear notes

A list of headings, subdivided with sub-headings listing the key points.

If you use linear notes, you can use different colours to highlight key points and keep topic areas together.

Use plenty of space to make your notes easy to use.

3   Try a diagrammatic form

The most common of which is a mind map.

To make a mind map, put the main heading in the centre of the paper and put a circle around it.]

Draw lines radiating from this to the main sub-headings which again have circles around them.

Continue the process from the sub-headings to sub-sub-headings.

Highlighting and underlining

You may find it useful to underline or highlight key points in your study text – but do be selective.

You may also wish to make notes in the margins.

Further reading

In addition to this text, you should also read the "Student section" of the "Accounting Technician" magazine every month to keep abreast of any guidance from the examiners.

Introduction to spreadsheet basics 1

Introduction

This chapter will guide you through how to open and close spreadsheets, guide you how to change name of workbooks/worksheets, and also how to save your work.

KNOWLEDGE
1.1 Identify what numerical and other information is needed in the spreadsheet and how it should be recorded.
1.4 Store and retrieve spreadsheet files effectively, in line with local guidelines and conventions where applicable.

1.1 Opening the application

There are numerous ways to open the application and the way that you do it will depend on the version of Excel that you are using and personal preference. We will follow the full path. From the bottom left hand corner of the screen:

EXCEL 2000	EXCEL 2003	EXCEL 2007
Start/ /All Programs/ /Microsoft Excel/	Start/ /All Programs/ /Microsoft Office/ /Microsoft Office Excel 2003	Start/ /Programs/ /Microsoft Office/ /Microsoft Office Excel 2007

Opening Excel 2003

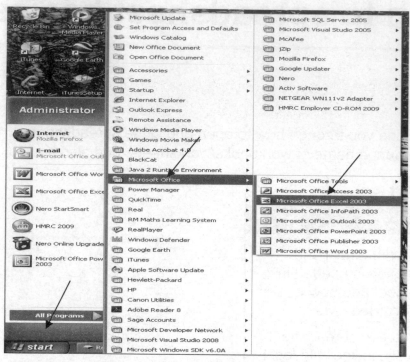

Excel will open:

- It will open a new **Workbook**

- It will be given a name by Excel, which will be changed later

- The workbook will contain 3 **Worksheets**. This is the standard default quantity, but this can be changed if you wish

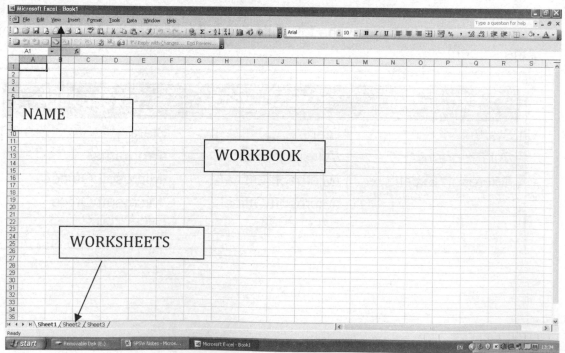

1.2 Opening an existing workbook

To work on a spreadsheet that has been previously saved.

- Open the application as above – then:

EXCEL 2000	EXCEL 2003	EXCEL 2007
File/	File/	Office button/
/Open/	/Open/	/Save as/
/Select location/	/Select location/	/Select Location/
Select file or folder/	Select file or folder/	/Select file or folder/

- The 'Open' dialogue box will appear
- Click on the down arrow to open the 'Look in' dialogue box
- Double click to open the folder that contains the workbook you wish to open
- Double click to open the workbook you have previously saved

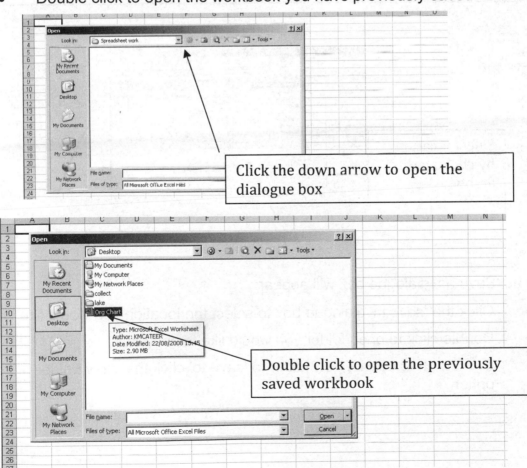

Click the down arrow to open the dialogue box

Double click to open the previously saved workbook

Shortcut

Control+o

Will reveal the 'Open' dialogue box

1.3   Saving the workbook

It is unlikely that you will want to keep the name that 'Excel' gives you at start up. You should therefore change the name to a more meaningful one and save our work in the location that you desire it to be in.

EXCEL 2000	EXCEL 2003	EXCEL 2007
File/	File/	Office button/
/Save as/	/Save as/	/Save as/
/Select Location/	/Select Location/	/Select Location/
/Select file or folder/	/Select file or folder/	/Select file or folder/

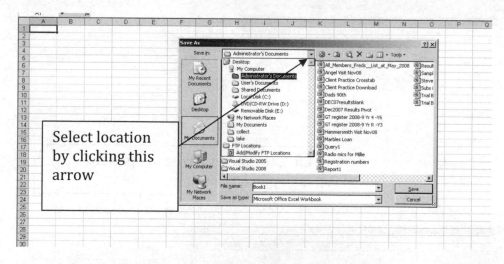

Select location by clicking this arrow

The 'Save as' dialogue box will appear:

- Click the 'save in' dialogue box to select the location you would like.

- Double click to open folder you would like to save to.

- If you wish to open a new folder to 'save to' click the 'New Folder' option.

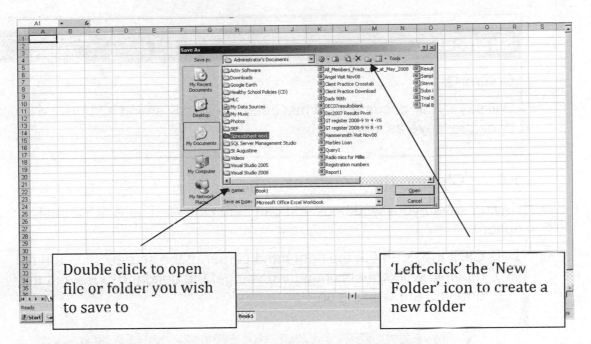

Double click to open file or folder you wish to save to

'Left-click' the 'New Folder' icon to create a new folder

- Create the filename you wish and click the 'save' button.

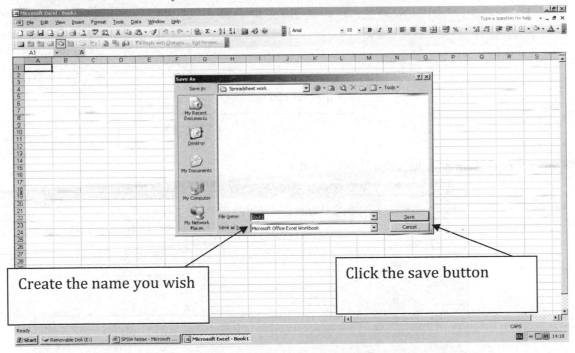

Create the name you wish

Click the save button

- Once the spreadsheet is saved you can save it again at anytime by clicking.

EXCEL 2000	EXCEL 2003	EXCEL 2007
File/ /Save/	File/ /Save/	Office button/ /Save/

Shortcut

Control+s

Will save your document if it has been previously saved. Otherwise it will open the 'save as' dialogue box.

1.4 Closing the workbook

Having saved your workbook you can then close it. There are 2 basic options:

1   Click the 'X' in the top right hand corner of the screen. [If you have multiple worksheets open then you get the option to close just the one you are working on.

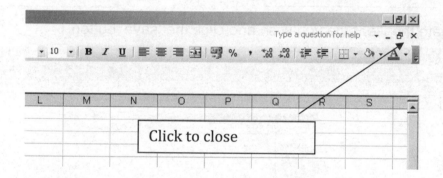

Click to close

2   Click 'File' and then 'Close'

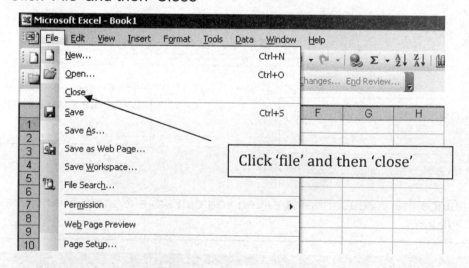

Click 'file' and then 'close'

If you haven't already saved the workbook you will be prompted to do so when you click 'close'. You can then follow the procedure above.

KAPLAN PUBLISHING

CAUTION !!!

If you close the workbook without first saving it you will lose everything that you have put into it since the last save. You are strongly advised to save your work regularly. /Drill down to the location of the workbook/

/'Right click' the workbook/

/Click 'Rename'/

/Rename your workbook/

1.5   Renaming the workbook and the worksheet

To 'Rename' your workbook you could:

(a)   Save the file using a different name

(b)   Or with the workbook closed

EXCEL 2000	EXCEL 2003	EXCEL 2007
Start/	Start/	Start/
/My Computer/	/My Computer/	/Open Microsoft Office Document/
/Drill down to the location of the workbook/	/Drill down to the location of the workbook/	/Drill down to the location of the workbook/
/'Right click' the workbook/	/'Right click' the workbook/	/'Right click' the workbook/
/Click 'Rename'/	/Click 'Rename'/	/Click 'Rename'/
/Rename your workbook/	/Rename your workbook/	/Rename your workbook/

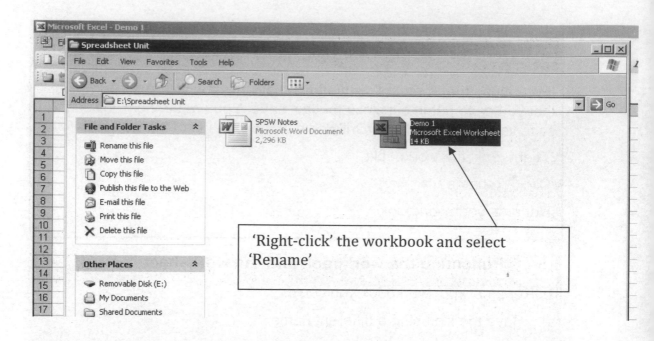

'Right-click' the workbook and select 'Rename'

Shortcut

On your keyboard you have a key with the 'Windows' icon

Click 'Icon+e'. /

Drill down to the workbook you wish to rename.

To 'Rename' a particular **worksheet** within a **workbook** you should do the following:

EXCEL 2000	EXCEL 2003	EXCEL 2007
	Format/ /Sheet/ /Rename/ /Type new name/	/Home Tab/ /Format Sheet/ /Rename Sheet/ /Type new name/

Shortcut

'Right-click' the tab of the worksheet and 'Left-click' 'Rename' the location of the workbook/'

/'Right click' the workbook/

/Click 'Rename'/

/Rename your workbook/

Student Activity 1

This **Activity** is case-sensitive so make sure you use Upper and Lower case where indicated. Do the tasks in Column order. Suggested answers can be found for all activities in your online Kaplan Engage access.

Column 1		Column 2	
Activity	Tick	**Activity**	Tick
Open the application		Save and Close the 'Workbook'	
Save the workbook as **LEARN1** in a folder titled **Student Solutions** on your C:drive		Go to **Student Solutions** and Rename **LEARN1** to **Activity1**	
Rename '**Sheet 1**' as MONTHLY SALES		Open **Activity1**	

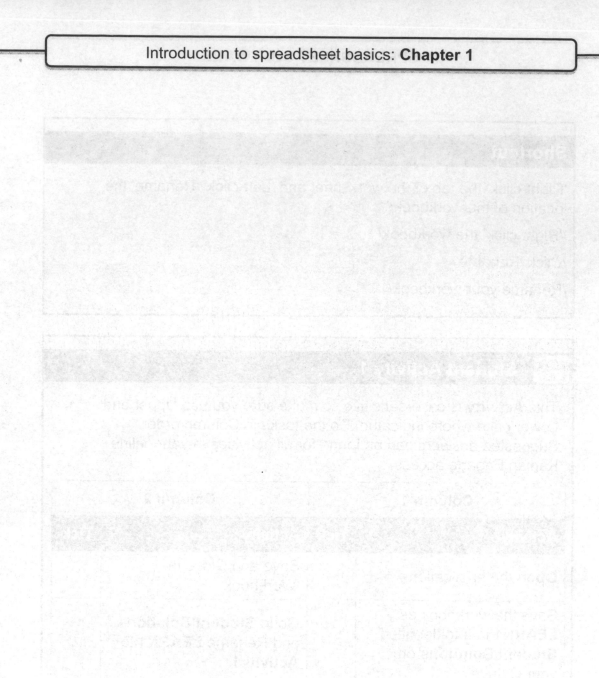

Getting started on your worksheet

Introduction

This chapter will guide you through the structure of the worksheet and how enter and amend data. You will also learn how to copy, paste, merge data and how to insert and delete rows and columns.

KNOWLEDGE
1.2 Enter numerical and other data accurately.

2.1 Spreadsheet structure

The spreadsheet [worksheet] shown above is made up of 'Rows', 'Columns' and 'Cells':

- The 'Rows' are numbered down the left hand-side from 1 – 65536

- The 'Columns' are lettered along the top from A – IV [256 columns]

- The 'Cells' are the junction of columns and rows [example cell A1 is the junction of Column A and Row 1]. There are 16,777,216 cells in a worksheet – far more than you will ever use.

- The 'Active' cell is where you are be able to enter data and is highlighted with a bold border [See B4 above]. Both the column letter and the row number are also highlighted

Shortcut

Control+home takes you to cell A1

Control+end takes you to the cell furthest into the worksheet that has been active [even if the content has been removed]

2.2 Entering data into your worksheet

Data can be entered into the 'Active Cell'. As this is done it will appear in the 'formula bar' and will stay there until you move away from the 'active cell'.

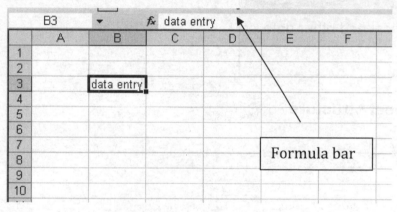

Data can also be entered into multiple cells. In the bottom right hand corner of the 'active cell' there is a little square block. If you hover over the block a 'cross' will appear. You can then 'click and hold' the left mouse button and then drag down, up, right or left to replicate the content of the 'active cell' in as many cells as you wish.

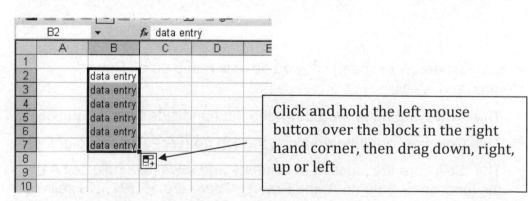

KAPLAN PUBLISHING

Shortcut

Excel will try and guess if there is a sequence involved in your data entry. For example weekdays, months, numerical sequences. If it can't find a sequence it will replicate exactly what you type into the 'Active Cell'.

Shortcut

Excel will not guess a sequence for a single number. If you enter two numbers into adjacent cells, then highlight both cells, Excel will continue the sequence that you created.

 Student Activity 2

This **Activity** is case-sensitive so make sure you use Upper and Lower case where indicated. Do the tasks in Column order.

Column 1		Column 2	
Activity	**Tick**	**Activity**	**Tick**
Go to **Activity1** that you previously saved in the **student solutions** folder on your pc and open it.		Replicate the sequence in Cells 'D5 and D6' down to 'D8'	
Save the workbook as **Activity2** in **Student Solutions**		Replicate the sequence in Cells 'D5 and E5' across to Cell 'O5'	
Type **January** into Cell 'D4' Replicate to Cell 'O4' by dragging to the right		Highlight Cells 'D6 – D8' and replicate the sequence to Cells 'O6 – O8' by dragging across	
Type **SALES1** into Cell 'C5' and replicate to Cell 'C8'		Save your work keeping **Activity2** as the worksheet name	
Type 100 into Cell 'D5' Type 110 into Cell 'E5' Type 130 into Cell 'D6'		Suggested Answers can be found in your online Kaplan Engage account.	

2.3   Copy, Paste and Paste Special

Excel allows you to copy data from the 'Active Cell[s]' to other cells.

EXCEL 2000	EXCEL 2003	EXCEL 2007
Edit/ /Copy/ /Paste/	Edit/ /Copy/ /Paste/	Home tab/ /Copy/ /Paste/

Shortcut

'Right-Click' the 'Active Cell[s]'. Click 'Copy'. Go to the cell[s] you wish to copy to. 'Right-Click and then click 'Paste. What you have copied will appear.

Shortcut

Highlight the active cells.

Ctrl+c will copy

Ctrl+v will paste

By holding the 'Control Button' down when pasting you can paste into non-adjacent cells.

There is another function 'Paste Special'. This function allows you to paste different aspects of what could be contained in a cell. Certain of these will be covered in later sessions. In the main what this function does is self explanatory. However, it is explained briefly below.

EXCEL 2000	EXCEL 2003	EXCEL 2007
Edit/ /Paste Special/	Edit/ /Paste Special/	Home tab/ /Copy/ Paste icon/ /Paste Special/

Shortcut

'Right-Click' the 'Active Cell[s]'. Click 'Copy'. Go to the cell[s] you wish to copy to. 'Right-Click and then click 'Paste Special'. Select what you want to happen.

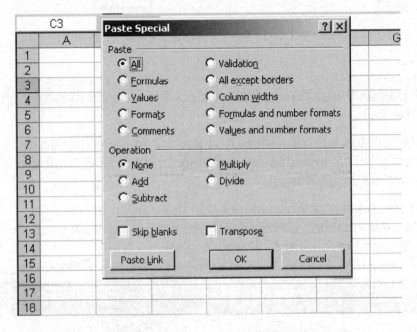

(i) **'All'** pastes content, formula and formatting but it will not alter column width

(ii) **'Formulas'** pastes the formula from the cell[s] to the new location. It maintains the structure of the formula but changes cell references accordingly – see example below. Note the formula in the formula bar. Do not worry about how formulas are written at this stage.

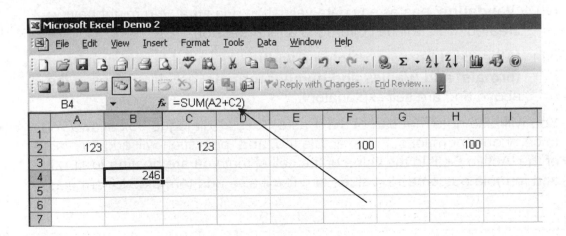

Here the formula in cell '**B4**' has been copied to cell '**G4**'. Again note the formula in the formula bar

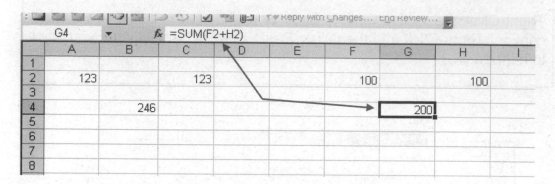

(iii) '**Values**' pastes the value of a cell and not the formula that may have created the value

(iv) '**Formats**' pastes any formatting that you might have carried out to the new cell[s]. This includes cell shading, borders and number formats, but not column width.

(v) '**Comments**' pastes any comments that have been entered into a cell to the new location. '**Comments**' allow you to write a note about a particular cell for you - and others - to see.

EXCEL 2000	EXCEL 2003	EXCEL 2007
Right Click/ /Insert Comment/ /Type your comment/	Right Click/ /Insert Comment/ /Type your comment/	Right Click/ /Insert Comment/ /Type your comment/

Once you have written your comment you will be able to delete and/or hide it by 'Right-Clicking' again in the 'Active Cell'.

(vi) '**Validation**' pastes any data validation rules that you might have created. This will be covered in a later session

(vii) '**All except borders**', '**Column widths**', '**Formulas and number formats**' and '**Values and number formats**' are derivatives of the above and are self explanatory.

You will also note that part of the 'Paste-Special' dialogue box allows you to carry out operations. For example the '**add**' operation will add the value of the 'Active Cell' to the value of the cell[s] that you are pasting to. It will add formula outcomes to values and it will also add formulas to formulas.

KAPLAN PUBLISHING

The last part of the 'Paste-Special' dialogue box allows two other actions

(i)   **'Skip Blanks'** ignores the content –formatting etc – of a cell with no data in it. However, it does maintain the gaps between non-adjacent cells.

(ii)   **'Transpose'** is a useful tool for pasting the content of a column into a row.

2.4   Editing, deleting and merging cell content

There are a number of ways to **edit** cell content.

1.   Go to the 'Active Cell'. The content of the cell will appear in the formula bar. 'Left-Click' into the formula bar and you will then be able to edit the content. You can use the left and right arrow keys to move around.

2.   You can double 'Left-Click' into the active cell. You can then edit the content in the same way as above

To **delete** cell content you can do the following

1.   Go to the cell you wish to delete. Press the delete key. You can highlight multiple adjacent cells and delete in the same way.

2.   'Right-Click' in the active cell and then 'Left-Click' **clear cell contents.** You can highlight multiple adjacent cells and delete in the same way.

3.   You can **delete** the content of non-adjacent cells by holding down the **control** key and 'Left-Clicking' the cells you wish to delete. Then press the delete key.

CAUTION !!!

If you 'Right-Click' a cell[s] and then click 'delete' Excel thinks you want to delete the cells completely. You will be offered a dialogue box asking you which way you want to shift the cells. This is a useful tool if it is your intention to shift data, but proceed with caution. You can always click 'Edit, Undo' or the undo icon on the toolbar if you change your mind.

You can **'Merge cells'**. This means that you can join a number of cells together to make one. This is a very useful tool for creating a visually attractive document. You should ensure that you can do this.

Again there are a number of ways to do this:

EXCEL 2000	EXCEL 2003	EXCEL 2007
Highlight the cells you wish to merge/ /Format/ /Cells/ /Alignment/ /Merge cells/	Highlight the cells you wish to merge/ /Format/ /Cells/ /Alignment/ /Merge cells/	Highlight the cells you wish to merge/ /Home tab/ /Merge and Centre/

Shortcuts

Highlight the cells you wish to merge then:

'Right-Click' then click 'Format Cells', click the Alignment tab and then click merge cells.

OR

Press control+1 and the alignment tab will appear.

OR

Click the 'Merge' icon on the Formatting toolbar

2.5 Inserting and deleting 'Rows' and 'Columns'

You can insert both rows and columns into your 'Worksheet'. Doing so will not increase or decrease the number of rows and columns in your worksheet. Excel will merely insert a blank row[s] or column[s] where it is told to do so and shift the other rows or columns down/right. Excel cannot insert when all rows or columns are in use – a very unlikely event – and it cannot insert if the last row or column are in use. You would need to delete a row or column from elsewhere first.

To add a row to your worksheet

EXCEL 2000	EXCEL 2003	EXCEL 2007
'Left-Click' on the row number where you would like to insert/ /Insert/ /Rows/	'Left-Click' on the row number where you would like to insert/ /Insert/ /Rows/	'Left-Click' on the row number where you would like to insert/ /Home Tab/ /Click 'Insert' icon/

Excel 2003

Excel 2007

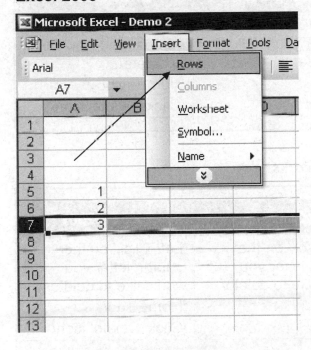

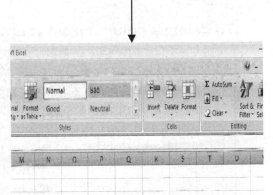

To add a column to your worksheet

EXCEL 2000	EXCEL 2003	EXCEL 2007
'Left-Click' on the column letter where you would like to insert/ /Insert/ /Columns/	'Left-Click' on the column letter where you would like to insert/ /Insert/ /Columns/	'Left-Click' on the column letter where you would like to insert/ /Home Tab/ /Click 'Insert' icon/

The same will happen as it does for rows, except that a column will be inserted and the other columns will move to the right.

Shortcut

'Right-Click' the row or column where you wish to insert, then click insert

To delete a row from your worksheet

EXCEL 2000	EXCEL 2003	EXCEL 2007
'Left-Click' on the row number you would like to delete/ /Edit/ /Delete/	'Left-Click' on the row number you would like to delete/ /Edit/ /Delete/	'Left-Click' on the row number you would like to delete/ /Home Tab/ /Click 'Delete' icon/

To delete a column from your worksheet

EXCEL 2000	EXCEL 2003	EXCEL 2007
'Left-Click' on the column letter you would like to delete/ /Edit/ /Delete/	'Left-Click' on the column letter you would like to delete/ /Edit/ /Delete/	'Left-Click' on the column letter you would like to delete/ /Home Tab/ /Click 'Delete' icon/

Shortcut

'Right-Click' the row or column you wish to remove, then click delete

OR

Highlight the row or column you wish to delete and then press 'Control+minus'

KAPLAN PUBLISHING

Student Activity 3

This **Activity** is case-sensitive so make sure you use Upper and Lower case where indicated. Carry out the tasks in Column Order. Suggested answers can be found in your online Kaplan Engage account.

Column 1		Column 2	
Activity	Tick	Activity	Tick
Go to **Activity2**		**Merge cells** 1.　B2 to D2 2.　E2 to G2 3.　H2 to J2 4.　K2 to M2	
Delete columns A and B		**Insert** a new column at **Column B**	
Save worksheet as **Activity3**		**Delete** Row 3	
Insert a row at **Row 7**		Type the following into. • Cell B4, John Martin • Cell B5, Jenny Manku • Cell B6, Roger Perwaiz • Cell B7, Mike Capstick • Cell B8, Sharon Newt	
In cell **A7** type SALES5		**Merge** cells A3 and B3	
Copy and Paste the Values of **Cells B5 to M5** into **Cells B7 to M7**		**Highlight** cells A4 to A8 and copy them	
Merge cells **A1** to **M1**		**Transpose** cells A4 to A8 into cells E24 to I24	
		Save Activity3 in **Student Solutions**	

Formatting your worksheet

3

Introduction

In this chapter you will learn how to change the visual appearance of a spreadsheet so that relevant data is shown. You will also learn how to use the correct formatting.

> ### KNOWLEDGE
>
> 1.3 Identify what numerical and other information is needed in the spreadsheet and how it should be recorded.
>
> 3.1 Explain how to present and format spreadsheet information effectively to meet needs.
>
> 3.2 Select and use appropriate tools and techniques to format cells, rows, columns and worksheets effectively.

Formatting is a process whereby you change the visual aspects of your worksheet. Your assessment will involve you in formatting worksheets to meet specific demands. You will in all likelihood be told what formatting is required and you will be assessed on whether or not you have complied with the instructions in the case-study.

The types of formatting you are required to be able to do are:

1 Adjust row height and column width

2 Add borders and shading to cells and cell ranges

3 Formatting text and numbers

3.1 Formatting rows and columns

Row height and column width can be changed to allow cell content to be visible. They can also be changed to allow a uniform size to rows and columns.

Adjusting column width

EXCEL 2000	EXCEL 2003	EXCEL 2007
Highlight the column[s] you wish to change/	Highlight the column[s] you wish to change/	Highlight the column[s] you wish to change/
/Format/	/Format/	/Home Tab/
/Column/	/Column/	/Format Icon/
/Width/	/Width/	/Column Width/

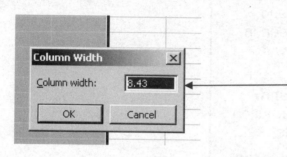

A dialogue box will open and you can then change the width.

Shortcuts

Highlight the columns you wish to change

'Right-Click' and 'Column Width

OR

Highlight the columns you wish to change

'Double-Click the dividing line between the column letters – you will get auto-fit for your cell content

OR

Highlight all the columns by clicking the junction point of cells and rows at the top left hand corner of the spreadsheet.

'Double-Click' any dividing line between the column letters – you will get auto-fit for the entire worksheet

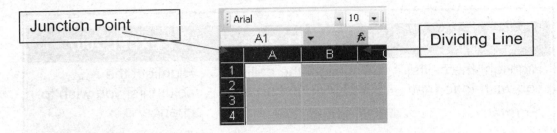

Junction Point

Dividing Line

Adjusting Row Height

This works in exactly the same way as above

EXCEL 2000	EXCEL 2003	EXCEL 2007
Highlight the rows[s] you wish to change/	Highlight the rows[s] you wish to change/	Highlight the column[s] you wish to change/
/Format/	/Format/	/Home Tab/
/Row/	/Row/	/Format Icon/
/Height/	/Height/	/Row Height/

Shortcuts

Highlight the Rows you wish to change

'Right-Click' and 'Row Height'

OR

Highlight the Rows you wish to change

'Double-Click the dividing line between the row numbers – you will get auto-fit for your cell content

OR

Highlight all the rows by clicking the junction point of cells and rows at the top left hand corner of the spreadsheet.

'Double-Click' any dividing line between the row numbers – you will get auto-fit for the entire worksheet

3.2 Adding Borders and Shading

EXCEL 2000	EXCEL 2003	EXCEL 2007
Highlight the cell[s] you wish to format/	Highlight the cell[s] you wish to format/	Highlight the column[s] you wish to change/
/Format/	/Format/	/Home Tab/
/Cells/	/Cells/	/Format Icon/
/Format Cells Dialogue box opens/	/Format Cells Dialogue box opens/	/Format Cells/
/Click relevant tab/	/Click relevant tab/	/Format Cells Dialogue box opens/
		/Click relevant tab/

Below you can see the Format Cells dialogue box. Note the different tabs that can be selected. You will use this dialogue box a number of times in this session to format other parts of the worksheet.

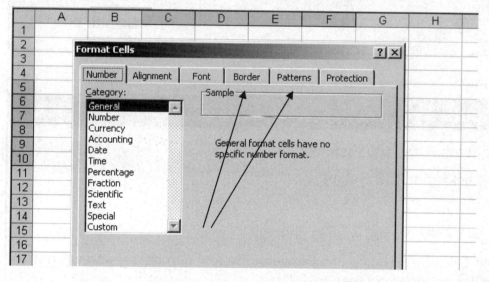

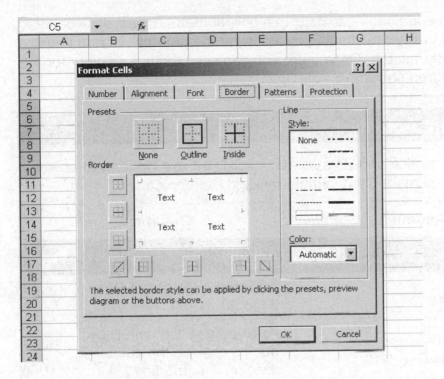

With the 'Border' tab opened you can now add borders to the cell or cells. You can create numerous types of border with different line thicknesses, styles and colour.

You can have different line thicknesses and colours in the same border if you wish. To create your border select your 'Style' and 'Colour' and then select the type of border you want.

Shortcuts

Highlight the cells you wish to format.

'Right-Click' and then 'Format Cells

OR

Highlight the cells you wish to format.

'Left-Click' the Borders icon on the formatting toolbar.

Select the border type you want. This does not allow you to change line thickness or colour - you have to accept the default. You can click on the 'Draw Borders' icon at the bottom of the borders dialogue box if you wish to change thickness or colour

It is common to add shading to cells to highlight them, especially when it comes to titles. We get to shading by following the path above and then clicking the 'Patterns' tab. Once there you can select either a colour for the cell[s] or a coloured pattern.

 Student Activity 4

This **Activity** is case-sensitive so make sure you use Upper and Lower case where indicated. Carry out the tasks in Column Order.

Column 1		Column 2	
Activity	Tick	Activity	Tick
Go to **Activity3**		**Adjust** the **Height** of Row 24 to 20	
Highlight cells C10-N10		**Auto-adjust** Column B by double clicking the column dividing line [the text should now be fully visible]	
Add a single thin border to the top of the cells **Add** a double thin border to the bottom of the cells		**Highlight** columns C-N and adjust the column width to 12	
Highlight cells E24-I30		**Highlight** cells E24-I24	
Add a thick RED outline border to the cells		**Add** a red shading to the cells	
Add thin RED inside borders to all the internal cell walls		Save worksheet as **Activity4** in **Student Solutions**	
		Suggested solutions can be found in the online access	

3.3   Formatting Text and Numbers

Formatting Text

Text entered into a cell will automatically 'align' to the left of a cell. 'Text' means any combination of letters and numbers. Numbers will automatically align to the right of a cell. Text or numbers entered into 'merged' cells will automatically align to the centre of the cells.

KAPLAN PUBLISHING

Excel will default to Arial, size 10, black and Regular. You do not have to accept the format that Excel provides and it can be easily changed.

EXCEL 2000	EXCEL 2003	EXCEL 2007
Highlight the cell[s] you wish to format/	Highlight the cell[s] you wish to format/	Highlight the column[s] you wish to change/
/Format/	/Format/	/Home Tab/
/Cells/	/Cells/	/Format Icon/
/Format Cells Dialogue box opens/	/Format Cells Dialogue box opens/	/Format Cells/
/Click relevant tab/	/Click relevant tab/	/Format Cells Dialogue box opens/
		/Click relevant tab/

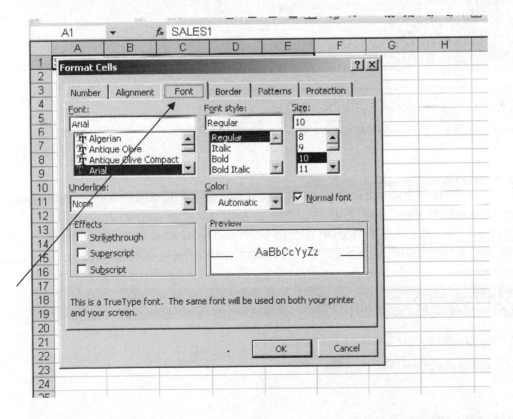

From the 'Font' tab you can choose a number of different effects. You can change the size, colour, style and also change the font itself.

You can also 'Underline' text. This is important to us because it is from here that you get the **'Accounting' double underline** that is used so often in accounting documents. The AAT have stated that knowing how to format using the accounting double underline is very important.

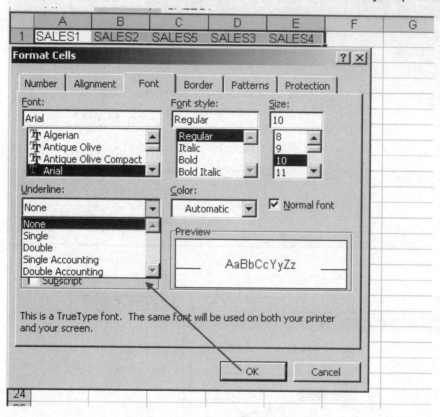

From the 'Alignment tab you can choose a number of different formats. You can choose to alter both the Horizontal and vertical alignment of the text. You can change the direction of the text and you can also choose to have the text wrap itself within the cell, rather than go on continuously.

Shortcuts

Highlight the cells you wish to format.

'Right-Click' and then 'Format Cells

OR

Highlight the cells you wish to format.

Click on the formatting icons at the top of the screen. However, you may find that you cannot always get all the options, especially underline and alignment

Student Activity 5

This **Activity** is case-sensitive so make sure you use Upper and Lower case where indicated. Carry out the tasks in Column Order.

Column 1		Column 2	
Activity	**Tick**	**Activity**	**Tick**
Go to **Activity4**		In cell A20 type. 'The region is divided into 5 areas. These areas are roughly the same size but do contain very different demographics' Make the text Font 12	
Highlight cells C3-N3		**Merge** cells A20-C21	
Centre the text in the cells and make the text **Bold**		'Wrap' the text in cell A20 and alter row height so that all the text is visible	
Highlight cells E24-I24		Alter the text alignment to the left.	
Centre the text in the cells and make the text **Bold** and **Dark Blue**		Alter the vertical alignment to 'Center' Highlight rows 20 and 21 and adjust the row height so that all the text is visible	
In cell A1 add the title 'SOUTHERN REGION SALES 2010'		Put a thick 'Blue' border around cell A20	
Make the text **bold, font size 14 and single underline.** If the text does not fit the row height, auto-adjust it		Save worksheet as **Activity5** in **Student Solutions**	

Formatting numbers

You will want to format the numbers in your worksheet to give the reader the best chance of understanding what you are showing them. For your assessment you need to know how to format the following:

1. Number of decimal places
2. 1000 separator [,]
3. Currency and Accounting
4. Percentages
5. Date and time formats
6. Custom formats

EXCEL 2000	EXCEL 2003	EXCEL 2007
Highlight the cell[s] you wish to format/	Highlight the cell[s] you wish to format/	Highlight the cell[s] you wish to format/
/Format/	/Format/	/Home Tab/
/Cells/	/Cells/	/Format Icon/
/Format Cells Dialogue box opens/	/Format Cells Dialogue box opens/	/Format Cells/
/Click 'Number' tab/	/Click 'Number' tab/	/Format Cells Dialogue box opens/
	/Defaults to number tab/	/ Click 'Number' tab /
		/Defaults to number tab

You are now presented with a list. From here you can select the number format you wish to have. When you click a particular format you will see that you are provided with a description of what the number format will give you.

General number format has no specific number format and Excel will not necessarily copy what you type into the cell.

Number, Currency, Accounting and Percentage all allow you to set a number of different format types and these are shown in the table below.

	Decimal Places	Negative number format	1000 Separator	Currency symbol
Number	Yes	Yes	Yes	
Currency	Yes	Yes	Auto	Yes
Accounting	Yes		Auto	Yes
Percentage	Yes			

Both **'currency'** and **'accounting'** formats allow you the use of the currency symbol, but only accounting aligns the decimal places and currency symbols.

CAUTION !!!

If you format a cell to say '2' decimal places and then insert a number with '3' decimal places, Excel will round the number you enter to '2' decimal places. However, when you use the cell content to carry out a calculation you will find that Excel will use the full number [all 3 decimal places] and you could find that you don't get the answer you expect or that it appears not to 'cast' [add up].

Similarly, if you calculate numbers that result in more decimal places than you format for, Excel will use the number that is calculated

Tip

You will find some but not all the numbering formats in the formatting toolbar at the top of the screen

Student Activity 6

This **Activity** is case-sensitive so make sure you use Upper and Lower case where indicated. Carry out the tasks in Column Order. Suggested answers can be found in your online Kaplan Engage account.

Column 1		Column 2	
Activity	Tick	**Activity**	Tick
Go to **Activity5, Highlight** and **Copy** cells E24-I30		**'Highlight'** and copy cells C6-C11	
Open sheet 2 and go to cell **C5**		Paste-Special, **'values and number formats'** into cells D6-F6	
Paste –special **Values and number formats**		**Highlight** cells D6-D11, then format cells to **'number'** to 1 decimal place	
Change the titles of cells C5-F5 to **General, Number, Currency and Accounting**		**Highlight** cells E6-E11, then format cells to **'currency'** to 2 decimal places	
In cells **C6-C11** type the following numbers		**Highlight** cells F6-F11, then format cells to **'accounting'** to 3 decimal places	
123.4 123.5 123.52 123.633 123.4567 123.99999		Clear content of cell **G5**. Save worksheet as **Activity6** in **Student Solutions**	

We will deal with the percentage format and how the numbers will calculate differently in Session 4.

Date and Time Formats

Date Formatting

Date formats are serial numbers that represent the number of days since January 1st 1900. This is how Excel can calculate the number of days lapsed between 2 dates.

Date formats can be accessed from the numbers tab as above. If you click on 'Date' you will be presented with numerous date formats and also a location. You should select English [United Kingdom] – if not shown.

Selecting a particular date format does not mean that dates need to be entered in this way. A number of different ways of writing dates can be entered and Excel will format it to your selection. You must, though, enter the year if you want any year other than the current year. If Excel doesn't understand the date format it will enter it as text.

If you enter a date into a cell Excel will create a date format. If you subsequently re-format the cell to a number or general, Excel will insert the appropriate serial number for that date.

Time Formatting

Time formats are also serial numbers. Here the serial number represents a fraction of a day. The day is based on the non-day of January 0 1900. To include just a time in a cell, click 'Time' on the number tab in the format cells dialogue box and select your time format. To get the correct time format you must put a colon between the hours and minutes, and the minutes and seconds for Excel to recognise what you are trying to do.

Date with Time Formatting

You can add a time to a date by first entering the date followed by a space and then the time in the 00:00 format. The time will only show in the formula bar, however, Excel will add the time as a fraction of the day and use it in any subsequent calculation.

Custom Number Formats

In the custom number drop down list there are a number of formats that can be changed by the user to a format of their own. Alternatively the user can create their own number format and save it here.

It is here that you can create a number format that allows you to have negative numbers in red with brackets representing the negative symbol. The format below would give numbers that have no decimal places and negative numbers would be shown in Red with a minus sign

#,##0;[Red]-#,##0,   **Result would be -1234**

You can change this to get rid of the minus sign and replace it with brackets

#,##0;[Red](#,##0),   **Result would be (1234)**

Student Activity 7

This **Activity** is case-sensitive so make sure you use Upper and Lower case where indicated. Carry out the tasks in Column Order.

Column 1		Column 2	
Activity	**Tick**	**Activity**	**Tick**
Go to **Activity6, Monthly Sales, Highlight** and **Copy** cells E24-I30		Type 13: into cell D6	
Open sheet 3 and go to cell **C5**		Type 13:10 into cell D7	
Paste –special **Values and number formats**		Type 13:10:30 into cell D8	
Change the titles of cells C5-F5 to **Date, Time, Date & Time, Serial Number**		Type 13 into cell D9, press the **End Key** and check the formula bar	
Make the text wrap for cells in Row '**5**'		Type 13.75 into cell D10, press the End Key and check the formula bar	
Delete the content of cell **G5**		Type 13, into cell D11	
Format cells C6-C11 into **Date Format** *14/03/2001, English (United Kingdom)		**Format** cells E6-E11 into **Date Format** *14/03/2001, English (United Kingdom)	
Type '**1**' into cell C6 and '**36526**' into cell C7		Type 1.5 into cell E6, press the End Key and check the formula bar	
Type 18 Jun into cell C8		Type 36526.75 into cell E7, press the End Key and check the formula bar	
Type Jun 18 into cell C9		Type 18/06 13:00 into cell E8, press the End Key and check the formula bar	
Type 18th June into cell C10		**Copy and Paste-Special** values and number formats from cells C6-C11 to F6	
Type 18-jun-04 into cell C11		**Highlight** cells F6-F11 and format the cells to **General**	
Format cells D6-D11 into **Time Format** *13:30:55, English (United Kingdom)		**Save** the workbook as **Activity7** in **Student Solutions**	

KAPLAN PUBLISHING

Simple functions for analysing data

Introduction

This chapter will explain to you how to create simple functions and to understand the order that Excel calculates.

> ### KNOWLEDGE
>
> 2.2 Select and use a wide range of appropriate functions and formulas to meet calculation requirements.

Once you have populated your spreadsheet with data you will need to format it to create information that can be used.

In this session you will be introduced to the following:

1. Operators and the order of Precedence

2. Parentheses (Brackets)

3. Simple formulas

4. Auto-sum

5. Calculation of percentages

4.1 Operators and the order of precedence

You are going to use simple mathematical functions to analyse your data but in order that you can do this you need to understand the order in which Excel calculates. Excel uses *operators* [each of which has a symbol] in these mathematical functions. Below is a list of the order of precedence. This is not the full list and later on during the course the full order of precedence will be shown.

Operator	Symbol	Order of Precedence
Multiplication	*	2
Division	/	2
Addition	+	3
Subtraction	-	3

4.2   Parentheses (Brackets)

The order of precedence determines which operators Excel will use 1st in its calculations. It can be seen above that Excel will 1st calculate a formula that contains multiplication or division.

Not only can you override this by using **parentheses** it is extremely important that you are able to do so in order that your calculations provide the correct answer [the one you intended]. By inserting **Brackets** around part of a formula it forces Excel to calculate the content of the **brackets** $1^{st,}$ followed by the remainder of the formula. You can have multiple sets of brackets in a formula as you will see in later sessions when you deal with more complex situations.

4.3   Simple formulas

Any and all formulas that you calculate must start with an **Equals** sign [=] otherwise Excel will not know what you are doing and treat your entry as text.

To highlight the need for putting brackets around numbers let us assume that you want to add together B4 and C4 and multiply this result by a 3rd number D4.

	A	B	C	D	E	F	
1							
2							
3							
4		4	3	5		=B4+C4*D4	

Without brackets Excel will give a total of 19. However, with brackets enclosing (B4+C4) you will get the result you require which is 35.

KAPLAN PUBLISHING

	A	B	C	D	E	F	
1							
2							
3							
4		4	3	5		=(B4+C4)*D4	

About the simplest formula that you can create is the SUM formula. You can use this formula to add, subtract, multiply or divide ranges of numbers and/or single cells.

4.4 Auto-Sum

Auto-Sum is a time-saving tool that Excel provides. It has quite useful functionality but it does not give you all the flexibility that creating your own formulas would. Auto-Sum is represented by the Greek letter Sigma (Σ) and is the mathematical summation symbol. It can be found on the standard toolbar at the top of the screen.

There are 5 options with auto-sum: Sum, Average, Count, Min and Max

- **SUM** adds a range of numbers

- **AVERAGE** calculates the average of a range of numbers

- **COUNT** calculates the number of items in a range of numbers

- **MIN** inserts the smallest number in a range and

- **MAX** inserts the largest number in a range

Student Activity 8

This **Activity** is case-sensitive so make sure you use Upper and Lower case where indicated. Carry out the tasks in Column Order.

Column 1		Column 2	
Activity	**Tick**	**Activity**	**Tick**
Go to Activity7 in your folder **Monthly Sales** sheet		In cell D25 type: Average In cell D26 type: Maximum In cell D27 type: Minimum In cell D28 type: Sales	
In cell **C10** type: =C4+C5+C6+C7+C8, press END key		In cell E25 **auto-sum AVERAGE** cells C4-N4 for SALES1	

In cell **D10** type: =sum(D4+5+D6+D7+D8), the press the Enter key		In cell F25 auto-sum Average for Sales2
In cell **E10** type: =sum Then do the following: Open brackets, and highlight cells E4-E8 and press the Enter key		In cells G,H and I25 calculate the Average sales for: Roger Perwaiz, Mike Capstick and Sharon Newt
In cell F10 click the Σ icon, highlight cells F4-F8 and press the Enter key		In cells E26 to I26 auto-sum the MAXIMUM figure for each sales person
In cell G10 type the following: =sum(G4:G8), and press the enter key		In cells E27 to I27 auto-sum the MINIMUM figure for each sales person
Copy the formula in cell G10 to cells H10-N10		In cells E28 to I28 calculate the annual sales figure for each sales person
Merge cells E22-I22		**Copy** and paste-special **Formats,** cells H24-H30 to cell K24. Type 'Totals' as a title in cell K24
Type into the merged cell 'Annual Statistics 2010' Format the text as **Bold** and font size 14		In cells K25-K28 auto-sum cells C4-N8 for Average, maximum, Minimum and Sales
		Save worksheet as **Activity8** in **Student Solutions** on your pc

4.5 Calculation of percentage

To calculate percentages you can use simple mathematical formula and format the cells as percentages. The percentage format can be found on the numbers tab of 'Format Cells'. Alternatively it can be found on the format toolbar as a **%** icon.

Student Activity 9

This **Activity** is case-sensitive so make sure you use Upper and Lower case where indicated. Carry out the tasks in Column Order.

Column 1		Column 2	
Activity	**Tick**	**Activity**	**Tick**
Go to Activity8 in your folder **Monthly Sales** worksheet		**Highlight** cells E29-I29 and format these cells to **Percentage** to 2 decimal places. Do the same for cells E30-I30	
The Sales Director wishes to know how each sales persons sales figures compare and asks for 2 things: 1 The percentage increase in sales for each salesperson from January to December. 2 The percentage of Total sales for each salesperson		In cell E29 type: =sum(N4-C4)/C4 Calculate the % increase for all the other salespersons	
In cell D29 type: Percentage Increase In cell D30 type: Percentage of Total Sales **Right Justify the text**		In cell FE30 type: =sum(E28/K28) Calculate the % of total sales for all the other salespersons	
		Save worksheet as **Activity9** in **Student Solutions** on your pc	

4.6 What happens with your numbers once you have formatted them.

The simple answer is that the number remains as it is entered or calculated and formatting it just changes the way that we view it. This means that formatted numbers can sometimes give a different result when they are summed, than they appear to give when viewed.

The simplest way to show this is by having a go.

 Student Activity 10

This **Activity** is case-sensitive so make sure you use Upper and Lower case where indicated. Carry out the tasks in Column Order. Suggested answers can be found online in your Kaplan Engage account.

Column 1		Column 2	
Activity	**Tick**	**Activity**	**Tick**
Go to Activity9 in your folder		Look at the solutions that Excel offers you	
Open sheet 2		If you add up the values that you can see in cells D6-D11 you will get the result 741.5	
In cell C14, auto-sum cells C6-C11		Whilst this is only a minor difference you need to be aware that with 100's possibly 1000's of cells in a spreadsheet it can make a significant difference.	
Copy and paste C14 to D14-F14		In a later session we will learn how to resolve this problem	
		Save the worksheet as **Activity10** in **Student Solutions** on your pc	

KAPLAN PUBLISHING

Page setup, presentation and printing 5

Introduction

This chapter will ensure that you are able to provide a document that is ready to publish and print showing only the necessary information that needs printing.

KNOWLEDGE

3.4 Select and use appropriate tools and techniques to generate, develop and format charts and graphs.

At some point it is extremely likely that you will need to publish or print your spreadsheets. In this session you will be introduced to the following:

1. Sorting and filtering data

2. Headers and Footers

3. Page Margins, Page Breaks and Orientation

4. Set print area

4. Print Preview and Print

5.1 Sorting and Filtering Data

At times you will be faced with large amounts of data. There will also be times when you would prefer to see only parts of this data or maybe you would like to view the data in a particular order.

Sorting Data

EXCEL 2000	EXCEL 2003	EXCEL 2007
Highlight the cell[s] you wish to sort/ /Data/ /Sort/ */Sort Dialogue box opens/*	Highlight the cell[s] you wish to sort/ /Data/ /Sort/ */Sort Dialogue box opens/*	Highlight the cells[s] you wish to sort/ /Data Tab/ /Sort Icon/ */ Sort Dialogue box opens /*

When the **'Sort'** dialogue box opens you will be faced with a number of options.

1. If your data has titles in the top row then you should click the **'Header Row'** radio button

2. You can sort by a number of levels – in either ascending or descending order

CAUTION !!!

You must be careful when sorting. If you exclude certain rows or columns when highlighting those for sorting, Excel will allow you to do this [sometimes you get an error message]. If you carry on and sort the data you will find that your data is out of sync. You can recover by clicking the undo icon on the toolbar at the top of the screen

If you get the data out of sync you will not get the results you were expecting from the data.

Student Activity 11

This **Activity** is case-sensitive so make sure you use Upper and Lower case where indicated. Carry out the tasks in Column Order. Suggested answers to these activities can be found in your online Kaplan Engage account.

Column 1		Column 2	
Activity	**Tick**	**Activity**	**Tick**
Open the **Eastern Region** spreadsheet from the list of files in your online Kaplan Engage account		**Open** the '**Sort**' dialogue box	
Go to the worksheet called **Eastern Data**		Make sure the '**Header Row**' radio button is selected	
Highlight the entire worksheet and auto-adjust the column widths		**Sort by** '**Salesperson**' ascending and '**Product Code**' descending	
Highlight cells A1-G97		Save the worksheet as **Activity11** in **Student Solutions** on your pc.	

Filtering Data

When faced with large amounts of data it is often beneficial to 'Filter' the data so that you are only looking at what you wish to see.

EXCEL 2000	EXCEL 2003	EXCEL 2007
Highlight the cell[s] you wish to Filter/ /Data/ /Filter/ /AutoFilter	Highlight the cell[s] you wish to Filter/ /Data/ /Filter/ /AutoFilter	Highlight the cells[s] you wish to Filter/ /Data Tab/ /Filter Icon/

Excel now inserts filter down arrows in the top row of data. If you change your mind you will find that the undo icon is unavailable. You need to follow the path that you have just taken and unclick AutoFilter.

You now have the option of filtering any or all of the columns. You can also carry out 'Custom' filtering. Here you get the option to filter in a number of different ways. Excel 2007 does have this option [Text filters/ Custom Filter]. However, as you are able to select multiple items from a column it is not really necessary.

 Student Activity 12

This **Activity** is case-sensitive so make sure you use Upper and Lower case where indicated. Carry out the tasks in Column Order.

Column 1		Column 2	
Activity	Tick	Activity	Tick
Open the **Activity11** worksheet from the **student solutions** folder on your pc		In column A [Month], **Filter Custom** **Month** equals **July** **OR** **Month** equals **August**	
Highlight cells A1-G97		**Highlight** all the visible cells	
Select **AutoFilter** [2003] or **Sort and Filter / Filter** [2007]		**Copy** and **Paste** the highlighted cells to : Sheet 2, cell A1	
In column F, **Filter** on **Eva Nasri**		Save worksheet as **Activity12** in **Student Solutions**	

This is a really useful tool if you need to extract just a certain amount of data. As you will see later in the session this tool can be used to quickly drill down into the data and print just what you filter.

5.2   Headers and Footers

Headers and Footers are used to provide information in a document such as document titles, data owner, version numbers, page numbers, dates etc.

EXCEL 2000	EXCEL 2003	EXCEL 2007
View/ /Header and Footer/ /Custom Header or Custom Footer/	View/ /Header and Footer/ /Custom Header or Custom Footer/	Insert tab/ /Header and Footer/ /Multiple options/

Once you have clicked Header and Footer you can elect to work on either the Header or Footer. In either you are given the same options. You can elect to insert something from a drop down list, or create your own **Custom Header** or **Footer.**

Student Activity 13

This **Activity** is case-sensitive so make sure you use Upper and Lower case where indicated. Carry out the tasks in Column Order.

Column 1		Column 2	
Activity	**Tick**	**Activity**	**Tick**
Open the **Activity12** workbook from the folder on your pc. **Eastern Data** worksheet. Select **Header and Footer** We will create our own **Header**		In the **Centre Section** type 'Page' [then push the space bar] **insert 'Page Number'** [then push the space bar] type 'of' [then push the space bar] **insert 'Pages'**	
In the **Centre Section** type 'EASTERN REGION DATA' Highlight the text and change the font to size 16		In the **Right Section** type 'Printed on' [then push the space bar] **insert 'Date'** type 'At' [then push the space bar] **insert 'Time'**	
Select **Custom Footer** [2003] **Go to Footer [2007]**		**EXCEL 2003** Click **OK** to close the Custom Footer dialogue box Click **OK** to close the Page	

		Setup dialogue box Check Print Preview	
In the **Left Section** type Version: 1.1 [enter key] Prepared By: Adam Smith [enter key] Date: 05/05/2010		**EXCEL 2007** **Click** View Tab Normal View Print Preview	
		Save the worksheet as **Activity 13** in **Student Solutions** on your pc	

5.3   Page Margins, Page Breaks and Orientation

Margins

To prepare documents so that they are visually pleasing – especially for printing – you need to set the page margins.

EXCEL 2000	EXCEL 2003	EXCEL 2007
File/ /Page Setup/ /Margins/	File/ /Page Setup/ /Margins/	Page Layout tab/ /Page Setup/ /Margins/

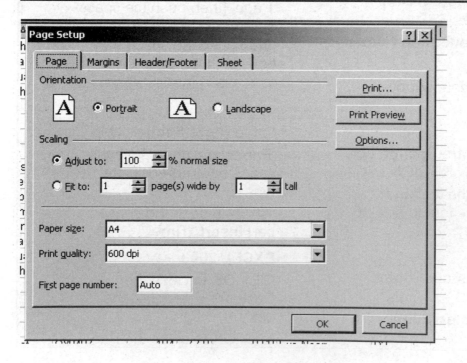

KAPLAN PUBLISHING

- With the dialogue box open you can alter the margins which will determine where on the page the spreadsheet will appear.

- You can also determine whereabouts on the page the Footer and Header will print.

- Additionally you can centre the content of the spreadsheet either horizontally or vertically on the page [or both].

- Once you have selected your margins these will be indicated on your worksheet by broken dashed lines.

Student Activity 14

This **Activity** is case-sensitive so make sure you use Upper and Lower case where indicated. Carry out the tasks in Column Order.

Column 1		Column 2	
Activity	Tick	**Activity**	Tick
Open the **Activity13** worksheet from your folder		Set the left and right 'Page Margins' to 2.4 and **centre** on page 'Horizontally	
Clear all the filters **Highlight** Row 1 and set the font to **Bold**		**Click** the 'Print Preview' button, then scroll down to the bottom of the page	
Sort the data by • Month • Product Code • Salesperson All ascending With the **Sort** dialogue box still open		You will see 2 dotted lines. Using your mouse cursor hover over the 2nd one up [page margin]. Your cursor will change shape. **Click and Hold down** the left mouse button. Now drag the dotted line up until it appears just above the 1st line of text. **Release** the mouse button.	
Excel 2003 **Click** the '**Options**' button **Select** the '**First Key Sort Order**' [2003] **Select** January, February, March etc [**OK**] exit from Dialogue Box		If the lines don't appear, click **margins** at the top of the page. There should now be enough space for the all the content of the footer to be displayed	

Excel 2007 **Select** Month **Click** Order, **Custom List** Exit from dialogue box		**Click** the **Close** button
Click 'Page Setup' then 'Margins'		Save the worksheet as **Activity 14** in **Student Solutions** on your pc

Page Breaks

With your margins set Excel will automatically insert a break in the data so that the right amount of data is displayed on a page. However, you will find that sometimes a natural break in the data is apparent and that you want to insert your own 'Page Break'

EXCEL 2000	EXCEL 2003	EXCEL 2007
Insert/ /Page Break/	Insert/ /Page Break/	Page Layout tab/ /Breaks/ /Insert Page Break/

Go to the row where you would like the **New** page to start. Highlight the entire row and then Insert/Page Break.

Student Activity 15

This **Activity** is case-sensitive so make sure you use Upper and Lower case where indicated. Carry out the tasks in Column Order.

Column 1		Column 2	
Activity	Tick	**Activity**	Tick
Open the **Activity14** worksheet from your folder		Save the worksheet as **Activity 15** in **Student Solutions**	
Highlight row 50		**Click** the 'Print Preview' button.	
Insert a page break		Check the result	
		Close 'Print Preview'	

Tip

Once you have inserted a Page Break, Excel allows you to view your document with the Page Breaks highlighted. When you are in this view you can move the page breaks around to suit yourself.

Go to View / Page Break Preview [2003] or View Tab / Page Break Preview [2007

Orientation

There are 2 ways to orientate your worksheet: Portrait; or Landscape.

Excel defaults to 'Portrait', but sometimes it is better to view your document in 'Landscape'. Viewing in this way allows you to view more columns [but fewer rows] on a page.

EXCEL 2000	EXCEL 2003	EXCEL 2007
File/ /Page Setup/ /Page/ /Select the view you want/	File/ /Page Setup/ /Page/ /Select the view you want/	Page Layout tab/ /Page Setup/ /Page/ /Select the view you want/

Student Activity 16

This **Activity** is case-sensitive so make sure you use Upper and Lower case where indicated. Carry out the tasks in Column Order.

Column 1		Column 2	
Activity	**Tick**	**Activity**	**Tick**
Open the **Activity15** worksheet		**Click OK** to the welcome dialogue box	
Click Page Setup / Page **'Landscape'**, **click Print Preview**		**Drag and Drop** the blue page break line splitting May so that it is between rows 33 and 34	

Note that 'May is now on 2 different pages as is 'November. **Click Close**		**Drag and Drop** the blue page break line splitting November so that it is between rows 81 and 82	
Click 'View' followed by **Page break preview**		**Click 'View'** followed by **Normal**	
		Save the worksheet as **Activity 16** in **Student Solutions**	

Tip

If you have inserted a Page Break that you wish to remove all you need to do is:

Highlight the row that contains the page break

Click Insert followed by **Remove page break [2003]**

Click Page Layout tab, Breaks and Remove Page Break **[2007]**

Set Print Area

Sometimes you may want to print only part of a document. This is a quite easy to do

EXCEL 2000	EXCEL 2003	EXCEL 2007
Highlight the cells you want to print/ /File/ /Set Print Area/	Highlight the cells you want to print/ /File/ /Set Print Area/	Highlight the cells you want to print/ Page Layout tab/ /Print Area/ /Set Print Area/

Student Activity 17

This **Activity** is case-sensitive so make sure you use Upper and Lower case where indicated. Carry out the tasks in Column Order.

Column 1		Column 2	
Activity	Tick	**Activity**	Tick
Open the **Activity16** worksheet		February data up to and including 'Sales Price' should be visible	
Highlight Cells A10:E17		**Close** Print Preview	
Click Set Print Area		Save the worksheet as **Activity 17** in **Student Solutions**	
Click the 'Print Preview' button		Suggested answers are found online	

 Student Activity 18

This **Activity** is case-sensitive so make sure you use Upper and Lower case where indicated. Carry out the tasks in Column Order.

Column 1		Column 2	
Activity	Tick	**Activity**	Tick
Open the **Activity17** worksheet		**Click** Set Print area	
Highlight Cells A10:E17		**Click** the 'Print Preview' button	
Click Clear Print area		February data up to and including 'Sales Price' should be visible, but this time you should have Titles	
Filter column 'A' for February		**Close** Print Preview	
Highlight Cells A1:E17		Save the worksheet as **Activity 18** in **Student Solutions**	

Print Preview and Printing

EXCEL 2000	EXCEL 2003	EXCEL 2007
/File/ /Print Preview/	/File/ /Print Preview/	Windows Icon/ /Print/ /Print Preview/

Having made all the adjustments to the data, format etc you will be in a position to print your document. Before you do this you should review it one more time – just to make sure. This is 'Print Preview'. When you are happy that your document is in the condition that you want it to be then you are in a position to 'Print'

Student Activity 19

This **Activity** is case-sensitive so make sure you use Upper and Lower case where indicated. Carry out the tasks in Column Order.

Column 1		Column 2	
Activity	**Tick**	**Activity**	**Tick**
Open the **Activity18** worksheet		Make the **Row Height** for Row 1 equal to 20	
Remove auto-filter		Format the cells in Row 1 so that vertical alignment is equal to **Top**	
Highlight the worksheet and clear the print area		**Underline** the titles in Row 1	
Click 'Print Preview'		**Right Align** the titles in columns C, D and E	
Note the following:		**Centre Align** the whole of column G	
• There are only titles on page 1 • The data is bunched tight against the titles • Quantity, cost and sales price figures appear offset to the title • Salesperson is bunched against sales price • There are empty spaces on pages 2 and 4		**Insert** a new column between columns E and F. Make the column width equal to 1	
		Format columns D and E so that they are 'Accounting' to 2 decimal places and without a symbol	
		Reduce the number of pages from 4 to 3 by moving 'Page Breaks' [there should be 4 months worth of data on each page].	
		Return to **Normal** view Save the worksheet as **Activity 19** in **Student Solutions**	

Cell referencing

6

Introduction

This chapter will guide you through the importance of referencing cells and how to create various types of cell referencing. You will also learn how to switch between viewing the results of our formulas and the formulas themselves.

KNOWLEDGE	
1.3	Combine and link data from different sources
2.2	Select and use a wide range of appropriate functions and formulas to meet calculation requirements.

In Session 4 simple formulas were introduced into your worksheet. These formulas were based on looking at the content of the individual cells and producing a mathematical answer.

You can create different types of formulae that use cell references to create the solution that you are looking for. This is particularly useful when you are using a particular number in a calculation that is used in different places and is also prone to change - such as tax rates.

There are three types of cell referencing that you have to be able to use for your assessment.

1.   Absolute cell referencing

2.   Relative cell referencing

3.   Mixed cell referencing

6.1   Absolute cell referencing

This is used to ensure that a formula always looks at the content of a particular cell. This means that if you were to drag or place a formula to/in a different cell – or range of cells – that Excel would continue to use that cell to calculate the solution. This is very useful for 'what-if' analysis when you are looking at particular scenarios.

To create an Absolute reference we use the $ sign thus $A$1.

6.2   Relative cell referencing

This is used when you are creating formulas that you would like Excel to change if you were to drag or place the formula to/in other cells. Excel will always keep the cell references relative to the original formula. For instance if you had a formula =(A1*B1) in cell C1 and you were to drag or copy this formula to cell C2, Excel would create =(A2*B2)

6.3   Mixed cell referencing

This is a combination of both Absolute and Relative referencing. Here you might want a Column or Row to be Absolute but the rest of the formula to be relative. For example:

If you placed =($A2*B1)in cell B2 and then copied this to cell C2 Excel would create =($A2*C1)

6.4   Viewing Formulas

It is very useful, and you will be called upon in your assessment to show in your document the formulas in the cells rather than the calculation.

EXCEL 2000	EXCEL 2003	EXCEL 2007
/Tools/ /Options/ /View Tab/ /Tick Formulas/	/Tools/ /Options/ /View Tab/ /Tick Formulas/	Formulas Tab/ /Show Formulas/

Shortcut

Ctrl+` [control and grave] will do the same as above. The same routine will also return you to the normal view.

Student Activity 20

This **Activity** is case-sensitive so make sure you use Upper and Lower case where indicated. Carry out the tasks in Column Order. Suggested answers are found in your online Kaplan Engage account.

Column 1		Column 2	
Activity	**Tick**	**Activity**	**Tick**
Open the **Referencing** workbook from your Engage account		**Highlight Cells** B4 and C4	
Open the **Absolute** worksheet		**Copy** the content of B4 and C4	
Format Cell B1 to **Percentage** to **2 Decimal Places** **Type** 17.5 into Cell B1		**Highlight** Cells B5 : B8 **Paste** the copied formulas	
In Cell B4 type =(A4*$B$1), press Enter key		**Right Align** the titles in columns A, B and C	
In Cell C4 type =sum(A4:B4), press Enter key		Save the worksheet as **Activity 20** in the **Student Solutions** folder on your pc	

Student Activity

This **Activity** is case-sensitive so make sure you use Upper and Lower case where indicated. Carry out the tasks in Column Order.

Column 1		Column 2	
Activity	**Tick**	**Activity**	**Tick**
Open the **Referencing** workbook again from your Engage account		**Paste the copied cells** into Cell I4 and then again into O4	
Open the **Relative** worksheet within Engage		**Note** how the formulas change **Relative** to Cells C4:E8	
Show the Formulas		**Highlight** the entire worksheet auto-adjust the column widths	
Note the construction of the formulas in Cells C4:E8		Save the worksheet as **Activity 20a** in **Student Solutions** on your pc	
Highlight Cells C4:E8 and **copy**			

 Student Activity

This **Activity** is case-sensitive so make sure you use Upper and Lower case where indicated. Carry out the tasks in Column Order.

Column 1		Column 2	
Activity	**Tick**	**Activity**	**Tick**
Go to **Page Set-up and the Page Tab**		Click **Print Preview**	
Orientate the worksheet to Landscape		Close **Print Preview**	
Click **Fit to** and **accept default**		Save the worksheet as **Activity 20a** in **Student Solutions**	

KAPLAN PUBLISHING

Student Activity

This **Activity** is case-sensitive so make sure you use Upper and Lower case where indicated. Carry out the tasks in Column Order.

Column 1		Column 2	
Activity	**Tick**	**Activity**	**Tick**
Open the **Referencing** workbook again from your Engage account		**Click** the bottom right hand corner of the **Bold** black rectangle and **Drag** this down to **Row 14**	
Open the **Mixed Referencing** worksheet		**Go to Options** and tick 'Formulas	
In Cell C3 type =($A3*$B$1)+($B3*C$2)		**Note** the construction of the formulas	
Drag the formula in C3 to D3:H3		Save the worksheet as **Activity 20b** in **Student Solutions**	
Whilst Cells C3:H3 are still **Highlighted**			

Conditional formatting

7

Introduction

This chapter will guide you on how to apply conditional formatting to cells based upon pre-determined criteria. You will also learn the different ways in which conditional formatting can be applied.

KNOWLEDGE
1.3 Explain how to present and format spreadsheet effectively to meet needs.
2.2 Select and use appropriate tools and techniques to format cells, rows, columns and worksheets effectively.

Conditional Formatting is used to format the contents of cell based upon a set of criteria.

EXCEL 2000	EXCEL 2003	EXCEL 2007
/Format/ /Conditional Formatting/	/ Format/ /Conditional Formatting/	Home Tab/ /Conditional Formatting/ /Manage Rules/ /New Rule/

FOR EXCEL 2003

A single Cell can have 3 formats and the formatting can be based upon the **cell value** or it can be derived from a **formula**. Conditional formatting is a 'Logical' function. This is because the formatting is based upon a True -or False result. If the condition that you set is true then the formatting will apply.

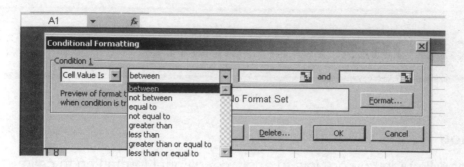

Above you can see conditions that can be used when 'Cell Value Is' is used.

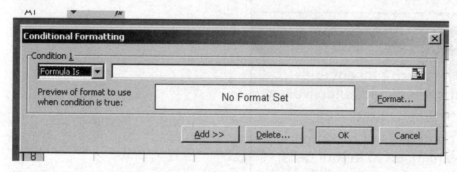

Above you can see the 'Formula Bar' into which you will have to enter your formula should you decide to set formats this way.

FOR EXCEL 2007

There are a number of **Conditional Formats** available in Excel 2007. We will look at only 2.

1.   Format only cells that contain

2.   Use a formula to determine which cells to format

These conditional formats work in exactly the same way as in Excel 2003, it is just the path that is different.

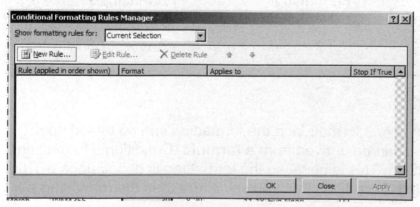

KAPLAN PUBLISHING

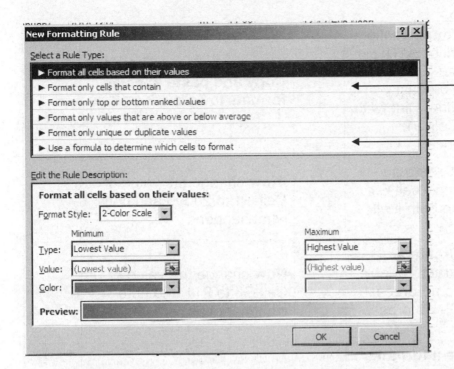

New Formatting Rule ? X

Select a Rule Type:

▶ Format all cells based on their values
▶ Format only cells that contain
▶ Format only top or bottom ranked values
▶ Format only values that are above or below average
▶ Format only unique or duplicate values
▶ Use a formula to determine which cells to format

Edit the Rule Description:

Format all cells based on their values:

Format Style: 2-Color Scale ▼

	Minimum		Maximum	
Type:	Lowest Value ▼		Highest Value ▼	
Value:	(Lowest value)		(Highest value)	
Color:	▼		▼	

Preview:

OK   Cancel

Student Activity 21

This **Activity** is case-sensitive so make sure you use Upper and Lower case where indicated. Carry out the tasks in Column Order.

Column 1		Column 2	
Activity	Tick	Activity	Tick
Open Conditional workbook in your engage account		**In Cell G6, Create a formula** subtract F6 from B6 – all relative	
Open the **Cell Value** worksheet in your engage account		Highlight cells B6 – G6 and drag the formulas down to row 13.	
Click into Cell B6 [active cell]		**Go to** Cell G6 **Conditional formatting** 1 Cell value = 0, format Yellow 2 Cell value > 0, format is light green 3 Cell value is < 0, format is Red	

Create a formula Multiply the 'Sales Price' by The 'Sales Volume {Cell G1}' so that the 'Forecast Revenue alters in line with changes to Cell G1 – mixed reference		**Copy and paste special formats** to cells G6-G13	
In Cell C6, Create a formula Multiply cell G1 by G3 – make both it all absolute		**Now** change the value of Cell G1 to 20000 and note what happens	
In Cell D6, Create a formula subtract Variable Costs [C6] from Forecast Revenue [B6]- all to be relative		**Now** change the value of Cell G3 to £11 and note what happens	
In E6, Create a formula make the cell value always equal to G2 [Absolute]			
In Cell F6, Create a formula 'Sum' cells C6 and E6 – all relative		Save the worksheet as **Activity 21 in Student Solutions** on your pc	

KAPLAN PUBLISHING

Student Activity 21a

This **Activity** is case-sensitive so make sure you use Upper and Lower case where indicated. Carry out the tasks in Column Order.

Column 1		Column 2	
Activity	**Tick**	**Activity**	**Tick**
Open Activity **21** workbook from your folder on your pc.		**Go to Conditional Formatting**	
Open the **Formula** worksheet		**Formula is** =D6=E6 **Format is** light blue	
Click into Cell D6 [active cell]		Copy, paste special, formats cells D6-D13	
Ensure G1 = 25000 G2 = £500000 G3 = £18		**Note what happens when** G1 = 20000 and then G1 = 20000 and G3 = £14 or £18	
		Save the worksheet as **Activity 21a** in **Student Solutions** on your pc	

Subtotalling

8

Introduction

This chapter will guide you on how to apply conditional formatting to cells based upon pre-determined criteria. You will also learn the different ways in which conditional formatting can be applied.

KNOWLEDGE
3.2 Select and use appropriate tools and techniques to format cells, rows, columns and worksheets effectively.

Inserting subtotals into lists of data can be a slow and laborious task. Excel has a tool that allows you to do this very quickly and with a minimum of fuss.

EXCEL 2000	EXCEL 2003	EXCEL 2007
/Data/ /Subtotals/	/Data/ /Subtotals/	Data Tab/ /Subtotal/

In order that you can subtotal the data list you will need to sort it first, as Subtotal calculates for **'each change in'**

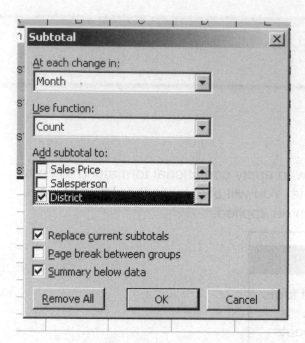

There are a number of different functions that can be used to calculate, with the default being SUM. If you are subtotalling non-numeric items then the COUNT function can be very useful.

You get to choose which columns are subtotalled – you can have more than one – and by ticking 'Summary Below Data', Excel will put the subtotal beneath the column.

You can create one set of subtotals and then run the routine again and select different items to subtotal. If you **deselect** 'Replace current subtotals', Excel will give you two sets of solutions.

If you wish to get rid of sub-totals, you can highlight the data, return to subtotals and then click **'Remove All'**

Student Activity 22

This **Activity** is case-sensitive so make sure you use Upper and Lower case where indicated. Carry out the tasks in Column Order.

Column 1		Column 2	
Activity	Tick	Activity	Tick
Open Activity 19 **workbook** from your folder			
Insert 2 columns between columns B and C		**Go to** Cell A1	
Cut and paste Columns I and J into the new columns C and D Delete column 'H' **Highlight** columns C and D **Right-Click** and then click 'Hide'		**Insert** subtotals, '**summing**' Quantity, Total Cost and Revenue	
In cell **H1** put a new title 'Total Cost. **In** cell **I1** put a new title '**Revenue**'		In the top left-hand corner of the worksheet select '2'	
In Cell **H2** create a formula that multiplies **Quantity by Cost** Copy the formula to the bottom cell of data in column **H**		Auto-size Column A	
In Cell **I2** create a formula that multiplies **Quantity by Sales Price** Copy the formula to the bottom cell of data in column I **Format** columns H and I, number to 2 decimal places		Save the worksheet as **Activity 22** in **Student Solutions** on your pc	

Panes, windows and split

Introduction

This chapter will explain to you how to freeze panes and show you how to view two or more worksheets side by side.

KNOWLEDGE
2.1 Explain what methods can be used to summarise, analyse and interpret spreadsheet data and when to use them.

9.1 Panes

When you have a lot of data in a spreadsheet and you want to scroll down or across, it is very handy to be able to 'Freeze Panes'. When you do this Excel will 'freeze' in position all rows above the 'Active Cell' and all columns the left of the 'Active Cell'

EXCEL 2000	EXCEL 2003	EXCEL 2007
/Window/ /Freeze Panes/	/Window/ /Freeze Panes/	View Tab/ /Freeze Panes/

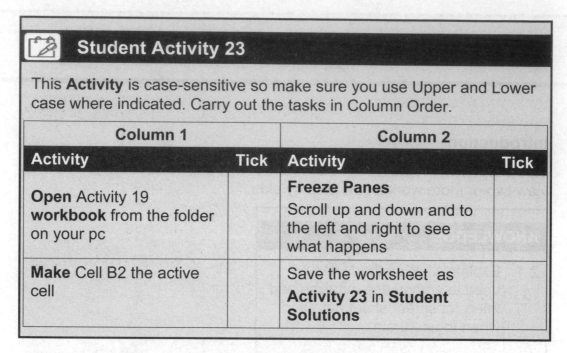

Student Activity 23

This **Activity** is case-sensitive so make sure you use Upper and Lower case where indicated. Carry out the tasks in Column Order.

Column 1		Column 2	
Activity	**Tick**	**Activity**	**Tick**
Open Activity 19 **workbook** from the folder on your pc		**Freeze Panes** Scroll up and down and to the left and right to see what happens	
Make Cell B2 the active cell		Save the worksheet as **Activity 23** in **Student Solutions**	

9.2   Windows

It is possible to view 2 or more worksheets at the same time. You need to open the worksheets that you want to view first

EXCEL 2000	EXCEL 2003	EXCEL 2007
/Window/ /Arrange/	/Window/ /Arrange/	View Tab/ /Arrange All/

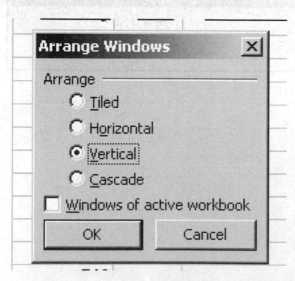

Horizontal and Vertical give you the best options. Using this method you get the opportunity to have one or the other of the worksheets as 'Active', and you can work and move around in it.

Rather than arrange, you can compare side by side. In this instance both the workbooks are active at the same time, so long as you have 'Synchronous Scrolling' turned on.

Student Activity 23a

This **Activity** is case-sensitive so make sure you use Upper and Lower case where indicated. Carry out the tasks in Column Order. Suggested solutions to all activities can be found online in your online Kaplan Engage account

Column 1		Column 2	
Activity	**Tick**	**Activity**	**Tick**
Open Activity 22 **workbook** from your folder **Open** Activity 23 **workbook** from your folder		**Click** into Activity 23, scroll up and down. **Click** into Activity 22, scroll up and down.	
Arrange windows Horizontally		**Close** both workbooks without saving	

9.3   Splitting a worksheet

This tool is used when you have a great deal of similar data in a worksheet and you wish to make a comparison to 2 different parts.

EXCEL 2000	EXCEL 2003	EXCEL 2007
/Window/ /Split/	/Window/ /Split/	View Tab/ /Split/

Once you have split, thick grey/blue bars appear on screen. You can move these bars around by hovering over them with your mouse. When the cursor changes, you can drag them where you want them. By clicking into a particular segment you can make it active.

You can reverse the split by going to Window / Remove Split [2003] or View Tab/ unclick split [2007]

Student Activity 23b

This **Activity** is case-sensitive so make sure you use Upper and Lower case where indicated. Carry out the tasks in Column Order. Suggested solutions are online.

Column 1		Column 2	
Activity	**Tick**	**Activity**	**Tick**
Open Activity 23 **workbook**		**Click** into the top right segment and scroll up and down	
Split the window **Drag** the thick bars around		**Close** the workbook without saving	

Sharing data

10

Introduction

This chapter will explain how to import data into different formats, how link data to other applications, and how to embed data.

KNOWLEDGE
1.3   Combine and link data from different sources.

10.1   Importing data in different formats

Sometimes we are given data that is not in spreadsheet format and will therefore not open up in Excel in the rows and columns that are provided. This data can be in a number of different formats. In this session we are going to look at data that come in a **delimited format**. Common types of format could be **Text** [.txt] or **CSV** [.csv] files.

Delimited data comes with characters such as commas or tabs separating each field. Excel will open these data formats but we need to do some work on them first before they are easily viewed.

EXCEL 2000	EXCEL 2003	EXCEL 2007
/Data/ /Import external data/ /Import data/	/Data/ /Import external data/ /Import data/	Data Tab/ /Choose the data icon you want/

Once we have asked Excel to 'Import Data' we are presented with a dialogue box so that we can choose the data file that we want to import. Once the file is selected we are presented with the following screen.

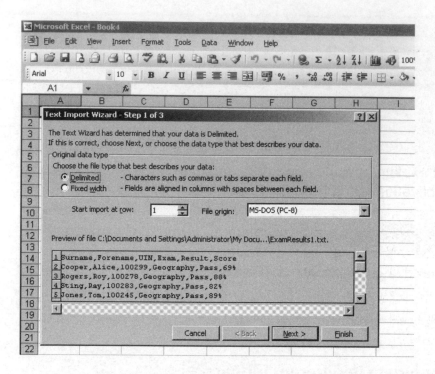

Excel will determine that the file is delimited and it is usual to accept that the wizard has chosen correctly and click **Next**. If your data file has unwanted rows at the top you can choose to have the import start at a particular row.

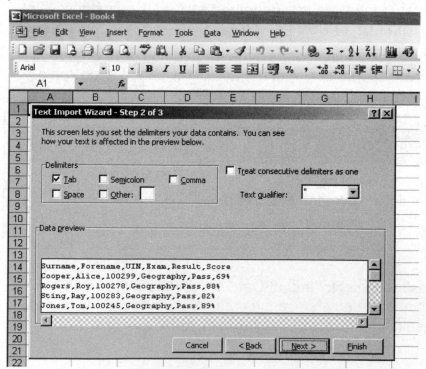

By looking at the data preview you will be able to see what type of delimiter the file contains and you can select this from the **'Delimiters'** offered. Sometimes you are given data files with consecutive delimiters. This means that there is a blank space. If you accept the default offered by Excel then you will be given an empty cell when the data is imported. If you click **'Treat consecutive delimiters as one'** then you will not get a space and the data will shuffle to the left. You need to be careful as you could get your data out of line if you choose incorrectly.

You can if you wish choose multiple delimiters. As soon as you choose a delimiter that Excel can recognise in the file then Excel will insert columns. If there are particular text fields they might have **'qualifiers' such as ["]** **or [']**. If this is the case you can alert Excel to this. In most cases you can simply accept the default. Once you are happy click 'Next'.

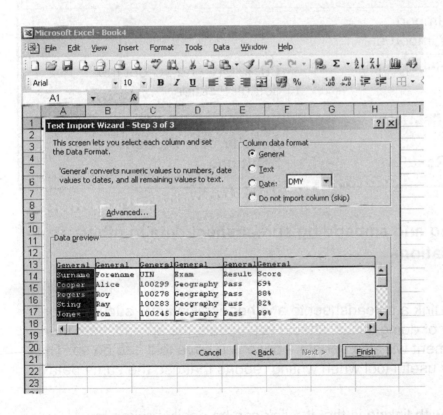

At step three of the wizard you can format individual columns. Unless you have a particular need you can accept the default. Once you are happy with your formatting you should click **'finish'**. Excel will now import the data into your spreadsheet.

Student Activity 24

This **Activity** is case-sensitive so make sure you use Upper and Lower case where indicated. Carry out the tasks in Column Order.

Column 1		Column 2	
Activity	**Tick**	**Activity**	**Tick**
Open a new **workbook**		Click **'Next'**	
Go to cell A1		**Insert** 'Comma' as the delimiter **Remove** 'Tab' **Click** 'Next'	
'Click' Data/ Import external data/ import data		**Click** 'Finish'	
Go to the Training Folder		**Click** 'OK' and accept the default location	
Insert **'Text Files'** into 'Files of Type' Open **'ExamResults1'**		Save the worksheet as **Activity 24** in **Student Solutions**	

10.2 Linking and embedding spreadsheet data in other applications

Linking Data

It is possible to link a spreadsheet to another application – such as Word. The advantage of doing this is, should you update the spreadsheet then the word document will also update – once you have told it to do so. This makes it a very useful tool when writing reports that use the same data frequently.

The drawback with linking is that the link can be easily broken by:-

- moving the spreadsheet to another place or
- renaming the spreadsheet.

If you break the link you will have to establish the link once again.

Embedding data

With embedding data you carry out the same activities as linking however you do not link the files. This means that the data will appear in the word document but it will not update if you alter the source spreadsheet.

EXCEL 2000	EXCEL 2003	EXCEL 2007
/Highlight the data you wish to link/	/Highlight the data you wish to link/	/Highlight the data you wish to link/
/Copy/	/Copy/	/Copy/
/Go to the word document/	/Go to the word document/	/Go to the word document/
/Edit/	/Edit/	/Edit/
/Paste special/	/Paste special/	/Paste special/

When the Paste-Special dialogue box appears you can choose whether you wish to just Paste the spreadsheet or if you wish to Paste and create a link. Once you have made your decision you should choose to paste a 'Microsoft Office Excel Worksheet Object'

Student Activity 25

This **Activity** is case-sensitive so make sure you use Upper and Lower case where indicated. Carry out the tasks in Column Order.

Column 1		Column 2	
Activity	Tick	Activity	Tick
Go to your online Engage account		**Go to** Doc1 Click **Edit, Paste Special**	
Open the **Doc1 WORD** document		**Paste** the data as an Excel object without linking	
Go to your engage account again		**Save** the word document as **Doc2** in **Student Solutions** on your pc	
Open the Eastern Region 3 workbook		Suggested solutions are found online	
Highlight and **Copy** cells A1-C17			

Student Activity

This **Activity** is case-sensitive so make sure you use Upper and Lower case where indicated. Carry out the tasks in Column Order.

Column 1		Column 2	
Activity	**Tick**	**Activity**	**Tick**
Go to the Eastern Region 3 workbook		**Go to** Doc2 **Right Click** into the 2nd table you pasted and click **'Update link'**	
Highlight and Copy cells A1-C17		**Note** the changes to the 2nd table. There is no opportunity to update the 1st table	
Go to Doc2 Move the cursor below the earlier paste		**Now** double click the 1st table. The table will change and look like a spreadsheet – you can now alter your table.	
Click **Edit, Paste Special**		**Now** double click the 2nd Table. The Eastern Region3 spreadsheet should now open	
Paste the data as an Excel object as a **linked** object		**Save** Eastern Region3 as **Activity 25**	
Go to the Eastern Region 3 workbook		**Save** the word document as **Doc3** in **Student Solutions** on your pc	
Change cells A2-A17 to **December**		Suggested solutions can be found online	

10.3   Embedding objects into Excel

It is possible to paste objects such as pictures and word documents into Excel. This is useful if you want to put a logo or picture into a spreadsheet. If you embed a Word document into a spreadsheet you have the facility to use the Word formatting tools. You can either import a blank word document or one that has been previously saved.

In either case you can choose to save the object as an icon. If you double click the icon the document will open. You can also choose to link to a previously saved document. This will allow you to view the most current version of the document. As before, you need to be careful about breaking the link.

EXCEL 2000	EXCEL 2003	EXCEL 2007
/Edit/ /Insert/ /Object/	/Edit/ /Insert/ /Object/	/Insert tab/ /Object icon/

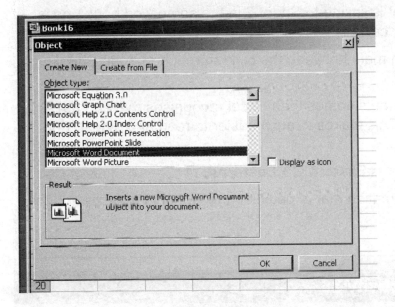

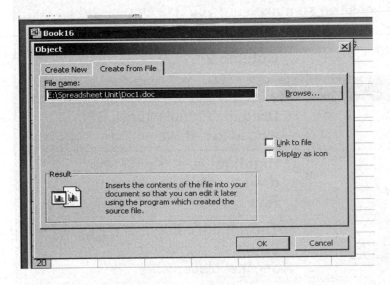

10.4   Linking to other Worksheets and Workbooks

It is very common for worksheets and workbooks to be linked. This can cut down the amount of work that needs to be done and it also means that spreadsheets can always be current.

Linking Worksheets

In the same way that we link cells together we can link worksheets. The only difference here is that we must refer to the cell in the worksheet we want to take the data from.

For example: suppose we want to link to 2 cells in another worksheet it could look something like this

=Sheet2!C8*Sheet2!E11

Here our spreadsheet is linking to Sheet 2 in the same workbook and is multiplying cell C8 by cell Ell.

Note the exclamation mark between the cell reference and the Sheet number.

If you give the worksheets names then Excel recognises this and uses them in the formula. This makes it much easier to read and digest. For example:

=Eastern!C8*Eastern!E11

Again *Note* the exclamation marks between the worksheet name and the cell reference.

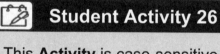 **Student Activity 26**

This **Activity** is case-sensitive so make sure you use Upper and Lower case where indicated. Carry out the tasks in Column Order.

Column 1		Column 2	
Activity	**Tick**	**Activity**	**Tick**
Go to your engage account		**Drag** the formula in cell B2 across to cell M2	
Open the 'Regional Combined' workbook		**Highlight** cells B2-M2 and **drag** the formulas down to Row 5	
Go to the 'Regional Combined Sales' sheet		**Format** the content of cells B2-M5 as number to 0 decimal places	

Click into cell B2 In this cell link together cell B2 from District 1 and District 2 by adding them together. **Hint** Once you have clicked into District 1 cell B2, click into the formula bar and add the + sign, then go to District 2 cell B2	**Apply** conditional format to cells B2-M5 1. where the cell value is greater than 1900 – format light green 2. Where the cell content is less than 500 – format bright yellow
	Save the Regional Combined workbook as **Activity 26 in Student Solutions** on your pc

10.5   Linking workbooks together

This is done in the same way as linking sheets, except that now you have to work with 2 or more workbooks.

When you link 2 or more workbooks together the formula will look something like:

='[Northern.xls]District 1'!$B$2+'[Southern.xls]District 2'!$B$2

The same rules on naming the worksheets apply but here NOTE the way that the workbook name and the worksheet name are included. This is because the workbooks already existed when they were linked and they were open. If you link workbooks together before they have been saved, Excel will apply the full path to the link when they are saved.

Note: also the absolute cell referencing that Excel has applied to the link. You have to be careful here and use the cell referencing correctly when linking. This means altering the cell referencing to suit.

Tip

If you have an absolute or mixed cell reference that you want to change

Highlight the cell reference that needs changing

Click the F4 button and you will see that the cell reference toggles between all the different combinations. Choose the one that you want

Student Activity 27

This **Activity** is case-sensitive so make sure you use Upper and Lower case where indicated. Carry out the tasks in Column Order.

Column 1		Column 2	
Activity	Tick	**Activity**	Tick
Go to your engage account		**Highlight** cells B2-M2 and **drag** the formulas down to Row 5	
Open the District Totals workbook Northern workbook Southern workbook		**Format** the content of cells B2-M10 as number to 0 decimal places	
Go to the 'District Totals' workbook		**In** cell B8 of the 'District Totals' worksheet, **auto-sum** the column B figures. **Add** a single line border at the top of the cell and a double line border at the bottom.	
Click into cell B2. In this cell link together cell B2 from [Northern]District 1 and [Southern]District 2 by adding them together. *Hint* Once you have clicked into District 1 cell B2, click into the formula bar and add the + sign, then go to District 2 cell B2		**Drag** this across to Cell M8	
		In Cell B10 auto-sum **Average** to create the average of cells B8-M8	
Remove the **absolute cell references**		**Save** the 'District Totals workbook as **Activity 27** in **Student Solutions.**	
Drag the formula in cell B2 across to cell M2		**Close** without saving Northern workbook Southern workbook	

Formulas and functions

11

Introduction

This chapter will look at the various formulas and functions that are used in Excel and you will learn how to evaluate and write and complex formulas.

> **KNOWLEDGE**
>
> 2.2 Select and use a wide range of appropriate functions and formulas to meet calculation requirements.

In this session you will learning when and where to use Functions, and how to insert them into formulas so that you get the results you desire.

The Functions that you need to know are:

- Round
- Lookup
- If, And & Or
- Date
  - Today
  - Now
  - Day, Month & Year

It is common for these functions to be used together to get formulas to work effectively and you will be doing this as the session progresses.

In an earlier session you were introduced to the order of precedence. In the table below is the full order of precedence.

Operator	Symbol	Order of Precedence
Exponentiation	^	1
Multiplication	*	2
Division	/	2
Addition	+	3
Subtraction	-	3
Concatenation	&	4
Equal to	=	5
Less than	<	5
Greater than	>	5

11.1 Round Function

In an earlier session you saw that you can format numbers to a number of decimal places. You also saw that Excel used the number entered into the cell and not the formatted number. This effect can lead to ranges of numbers not necessarily adding up as you view them. To overcome this you can use the **Round** function.

The **Round** function allows you to determine how many digits you desire in a number, Excel will then round the number mathematically.

The **Round** function is written thus:

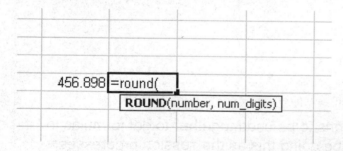

As you type in the function Excel will offer you some guidance. For this function you need the number to be rounded – usually a cell reference, followed by a comma and then the number of digits that you wish to round to. As with any function it must start with an 'equals' sign and the **'arguments'** must be inside parentheses [brackets].

Example

	D	Formula	Solution
6	456.84712345	=ROUND(D6,7)	456.8471235
7	456.84712345	=ROUND(D7,6)	456.847123
8	456.84712345	=ROUND(D8,4)	456.8471
9	456.84712345	=ROUND(D9,3)	456.847
10	456.84712345	=ROUND(D10,2)	456.85
11	456.84712345	=ROUND(D11,1)	456.8

	D	Formula	Solution
6	-456.84712345	=ROUND(D6,7)	-456.8471235
7	-456.84712345	=ROUND(D7,6)	-456.847123
8	-456.84712345	=ROUND(D8,4)	-456.8471
9	-456.84712345	=ROUND(D9,3)	-456.847
10	-456.84712345	=ROUND(D10,2)	-456.85
11	-456.84712345	=ROUND(D11,1)	-456.8

If you specifically wish to round up or down then there are functions for this as well

	D	Formula	Solution
6	456.84712345	=ROUNDDOWN(D6,7)	456.8471234
7	456.84712345	=ROUNDDOWN(D7,6)	456.847123
8	456.84712345	=ROUNDDOWN(D8,4)	456.8471
9	456.84712345	=ROUNDDOWN(D9,3)	456.847
10	456.84712345	=ROUNDDOWN(D10,2)	456.84
11	456.84712345	=ROUNDDOWN(D11,1)	456.8

	D	Formula	Solution
6	456.84712345	=ROUNDUP(D6,7)	456.8471235
7	456.84712345	=ROUNDUP(D7,6)	456.847124
8	456.84712345	=ROUNDUP(D8,4)	456.8472
9	456.84712345	=ROUNDUP(D9,3)	456.848
10	456.84712345	=ROUNDUP(D10,2)	456.85
11	456.84712345	=ROUNDUP(D11,1)	456.9

Student Activity 28

This **Activity** is case-sensitive so make sure you use Upper and Lower case where indicated. Carry out the tasks in Column Order. Suggested solutions are found online.

Column 1		Column 2	
Activity	**Tick**	**Activity**	**Tick**
Go to your engage account		**In** cell C17, create a formula to calculate the cost per unit. Divide **Full production cost** by **Production**	
Open 'Cost of production' workbook		**Copy** the above formula into cells D17 and E17	
Go to cell C11		**In cell C20** use the **'Round'** function to round the result in cell C17 to 2 decimal places =Round(C17,2)	
Create a **formula** that multiplies cells (B3 by C6) and then multiply this by cell C2. Once complete you must copy this formula to cells D11 and E11		**Copy** this formula to cells D17 and E17	
Note you will require a mixture of absolute and mixed references, to ensure that the formula works properly. Cell B3 would need to be absolute and cells C6 and C2 would need to be mixed to ensure that you are multiplying the correct column and that the row will not change		**Save** the workbook as **Activity 28** in **Student Solutions**	

KAPLAN PUBLISHING

11.2   Lookup Function

There are 3 basic Lookup functions that allow you to Look Up a value in one column or row and then return another value from another column or row.

The three basic functions are:

- LOOKUP
- VLOOKUP
- HLOOKUP

LOOKUP

This function looks up a value in one column or row range and returns a value from the same position in another row or column range. These ranges are known as **vectors**.

The **LOOKUP** function is written thus:

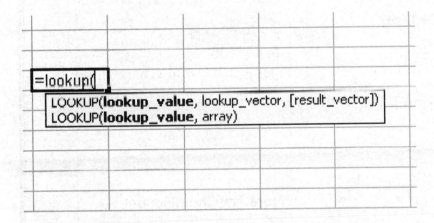

The **LOOKUP** function will require a **lookup-value** usually a cell reference, followed by a comma. It then needs the **lookup range**, followed by a comma. Then the function requires the **result range**. As usual the arguments must be encased in parentheses.

When the formula is complete it will look something like this:

=LOOKUP(C1,C12:C36,D12:D36)

- If the look up value is less than lowest value in the range then #N/A will be returned.

- If the look up value is higher than the highest value in the range then the highest value in the result range will be returned

- The lookup range must be sorted in **ascending** order

Student Activity 29

This **Activity** is case-sensitive so make sure you use Upper and Lower case where indicated. Carry out the tasks in Column Order. Suggested solutions are found online.

Column 1		Column 2	
Activity	Tick	Activity	Tick
Go to your Engage		**Go to** cell C2 **Type** KJ3935	
Open the '**Price Lookup**' workbook		**Go to** cell C3 **Type** 10	
Go to cell D4		**Note** how the values in cells D4, F4 and H4 change	
Type =LOOKUP(C2, **Select** range C13:C37 **comma** **Select** range D13:D37 **comma** **Close** Brackets **Enter**		**Go to** cell C4 **Type** 100	
Go to cell F4 **Create** a LOOKUP formula You are to look up the value in cell C4. The look up range is H13:H24 and the result range is I13:I24		**Note** how the discount % remains at 13	
Go to cell H4 **Create** a formula You need to multiply the list price in cell D4 by (100% minus the Discount % in F4)		**Save** the workbook as **Activity 29** in **Student Solutions**	

VLOOKUP

This function looks up the value in the **first** column of the look up table and returns a value from specific column in the table. The look up table is arranged vertically.

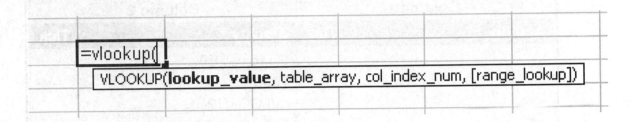

The **VLOOKUP** function will require :

- A look up value – usually a cell reference, followed by a comma.

- The cell references of the lookup table, followed by a comma.

- The column number from where the result is to be taken.

- An **Optional** range lookup value **true** [or omitted] and **false**

  - If the range value is set to **true** or omitted, then the function will return the next lowest value if it can't find the actual look up value.

  - If the range lookup is set to **true** or omitted then the **first** column of the lookup table must be sorted in ascending order.

  - If the range lookup is set to **true** or omitted and the look up value is less than the lowest value in the lookup table then the function will return **#N/A**

  - If the range value is set to **false**, then the function will search for an exact match. If it cannot find an exact match the function will return **#N/A**.

  - If the range value is set to **false** then the **first** column of the lookup table does not need to be sorted in ascending order.

Student Activity 30

This **Activity** is case-sensitive so make sure you use Upper and Lower case where indicated. Carry out the tasks in Column Order.

Column 1		Column 2	
Activity	**Tick**	**Activity**	**Tick**
Go to your engage account		**Go to** cell E9 **Type** =VLOOKUP(**Select** cell D5 **comma** **Go to** 'Lookup Table' worksheet **Select cells** A1:E8 **comma** **Enter** column number for 'Commission' **4 comma** **Type** True and **Close** brackets **Type** *D5 **Enter**	
Open the **'Salary VLookup'** workbook		**Go to** cell F9 **Create** a VLOOKUP formula to calculate the **Bonus** **Note** this is a % of the **Sales Figure**	
Go to the **'Salary Calculator'** worksheet		**Go to** cell G9 **Create** a formula to sum the values in cells D9:F9	
Go to cell D9 **Type** =VLOOKUP(**Select** cell D5 **comma** **Go to** 'Lookup Table' worksheet **Select cells** A1:E8 **comma** **Enter** column number for 'Basic Wage' **3 comma** **Type** True and **Close** brackets **Enter**		**Enter** some figures into cell D5 and see what happens **Save** the workbook as **Activity 30** in **Student Solutions**	

KAPLAN PUBLISHING

HLOOKUP

This function works in exactly the same way as the **VLOOKUP** function in every way. The difference is that for **HLOOKUP**

- the look up table is arranged **horizontally**
- and our lookup range and results range are in rows and not columns

Student Activity 31

This **Activity** is case-sensitive so make sure you use Upper and Lower case where indicated. Carry out the tasks in Column Order.

Column 1		Column 2	
Activity	Tick	**Activity**	Tick
Go to your engage account		**Go to** cell E9 **Create** a HLOOKUP formula to calculate the **Commission** **Note** this is a % of the **Sales Figure**	
Open the 'Salary HLookup' workbook		**Go to** cell F9 **Create** a HLOOKUP formula to calculate the **Bonus** **Note** this is a % of the **Basic Figure**	
Go to the 'Salary Calculator' worksheet		**Go to** cell G9 **Create** a formula to sum the values in cells D9:F9	
Go to cell D9 **Type** =HLOOKUP(**Select** cell D5 **comma** **Go to** 'Lookup Table' worksheet **Select cells** A2:H6 **comma** **Enter** row number for 'Basic Wage' **3 comma** **Type** True and **Close** brackets **Enter**		**Enter** some figures into cell D5 and see what happens Delete the content of cell D5 **Save** the workbook as **Activity 31** in **Student Solutions**	

11.3   IF, AND & OR Functions

All of these functions are known as Logical Functions. This means that the functions will prove a **True** or **False** result for the formula that they are in. It is very common for these functions to be used together in the same formula.

IF Function

This function is used to test for some form of result. If the result turns out to be **true** then the formula will do one thing and if the result is **false** then it will do something else. It is possible to have more than one IF function in a formula. These are known as **nested IF** functions. You are allowed a maximum of 7 **nested IFs**.

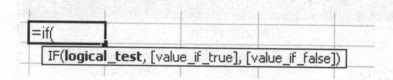

The IF function could resemble the one below. Here you are testing to see if the value of Cell D2 is greater than or equal to 45000. If the result is **true** then Happy will appear in the active cell. If the result is **false** then Sad will appear in the active cell.

Note: when using text values in **IF** functions you need to enclose the text in **speech marks [""]**

=IF(D2>=45000,"Happy","Sad")

Of course you do not need to use text values, you could just as easily use numbers or cell references.

If you need to use a **nested** IF function then it will look something like the one below

IF(D2>65000,"Minted",IF(D2>45000,"Happy","Sad"))

Note here the order. The IF function works from outside to in and will give a result as it finds it. This means that if we wrote the function this way:

IF(D2>45000,"Happy",IF(D2>65000,"Minted","Sad"))

then any number greater than 45000 in Cell D2 would give the result Happy. It would ignore the 65000 argument.

Note also the use of brackets. You must enclose – as normal – our functions with brackets but you must also nest the bracket inside. You must have the same number of left brackets **[( ]** as right brackets **[ )]**

You can combine your IF functions to create other formulas. For example

=SUM(IF(D2>45000,D2,0)+IF(D5<30000,D5,0)

Here if the arguments in D2 and/or D5 were true their values in these cells would be included in the sum. If the argument in either cell was false then the number added from that cell would be 0.

 Student Activity 32

This **Activity** is case-sensitive so make sure you use Upper and Lower case where indicated. Carry out the tasks in Column Order. Solutions are found online.

Column 1		Column 2	
Activity	**Tick**	**Activity**	**Tick**
Go to your Student Solutions folder on your pc		**Go to** cell D9 **Type** =IF(D5>0 **comma** **Create** the HLookup formula again HLOOKUP(D5,'Lookup Table'!A2:H6,3,TRUE) **Type** comma 0) **Result is** =IF(D5>0,HLOOKUP(D5,'Lookup Table'!A2:H6,3,TRUE),0)	
Open the 'Activity 31 workbook		**Go to** cells E9 and F9 and create an IF formula around the lookups	
Go to the 'Salary Calculator' worksheet Make sure that cell D5 is clear		**Enter** some figures into cell D5 and see what happens	
Note in cells D9:G9 that each cell says **#N/A**. This means that data is not available **We need** to create an **IF** formula to remove this.		**Save** the workbook as **Activity 32** in **Student Solutions**	

Student Activity 33

This **Activity** is case-sensitive so make sure you use Upper and Lower case where indicated. Carry out the tasks in Column Order.

Column 1		Column 2	
Activity	**Tick**	**Activity**	**Tick**
Go to the your Engage account		**In** row 15 sum the totals by product	
Open the **Boat Sales** workshop **Go to** Monthly Sales worksheet Cell D10		**Go to** cell I10 **Using** the **IF** function create a formula that removes the customer discount from **Total Sales** assuming the customer reaches their **Volume Target** for the period. **Note** this is the **Total** sales volume for the customer If no discount is allowed the cell should show **total sales**	
Create a formula that calculates the sales volume × pricing for the product within customer Give regard to relative and absolute references ='Sales Volume'!C6*Pricing!C$6		**Copy** the formula to other relevant cells, make sure that referencing is accurate 'if necessary'	
Copy this formula to all other relevant cells		**Go to** cells J10-J13 **Create** a formula using the IF function that shows the statement "No discount allowed" if discount for the customer is zero. The cell should remain **blank** otherwise	
In column H, **create** a formula to sum the total sales by customer		**Save** the workbook as **Activity 33** in **Student Solutions**	

AND Function

The **AND** function is also a **logical** function. It gives a **true** or **false** solution to 2 or more **arguments**. The function requires that all the arguments are correct to provide **true** as the solution. If any of the arguments are incorrect then the solution will be **false**. This function is commonly used in conjunction with other functions –such as **IF**.

The function is built thus:

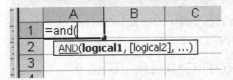

Below are two examples: example one shows the result if January and February are both equal to, or greater than 500; example two is the same formula but February is only 300 so the result is false

January	February		
500	700	=AND(B2>=500,C2>=500)	TRUE
January	February		
500	300	=AND(B6>=500,C6>=500)	FALSE

It is very common to use the **AND** function in **IF** statements. When you do this the outcome for the **IF** formula is based on the result of the **AND** function, thus:

=IF(AND(B2>=500,C2>=500), "Improving","Disappointing")

The above **IF** statement would result in **Improving** if the result was that January and February were both equal to, or greater than 500.

If - as in example 2 – January or February [or both] were less than 500, then **Disappointing** would be the result.

You are not limited by the number of **logical values** you put in your **AND** function as the example below shows.

January	February	March	April		
500	700	410	410	=AND(B2>=500,C2>=500,D2>400,E2>400)	TRUE
January	February	March	April		
500	300	410	400	=AND(B6>=500,C6>=500,D6>400,E6>400)	FALSE

Student Activity 34

This **Activity** is case-sensitive so make sure you use Upper and Lower case where indicated. Carry out the tasks in Column Order.

Column 1		Column 2	
Activity	**Tick**	**Activity**	**Tick**
Go to your Engage account		**In** row 15 sum the totals by product	
Open the **Boat Sales Two** workbook **Go to** Monthly Sales worksheet Cell D10		**Go to** cell G10, **create** an IF formula combined with the AND function that calculates discount. The result **MUST** be that discount is not allowed unless the customer reaches their target volume in boat sales of all types. If discount is not allowed then discounted sales must be equal to total sales	
Create a formula that calculates the monthly sales by multiplying sales volume by pricing. This is to be done by customer within product. Give regard to cell referencing		**Copy** the formula to other relevant cells, make sure that referencing is accurate 'if necessary'	
Copy this formula to all other relevant cells		**Go to** cell H10 **Create** a formula using the IF function that shows the statement "Target volume not met" if discount for the customer is zero. The cell should state "Discount allowed" otherwise	
In column F, **create** a formula to sum the total sales by customer		**Save** the workbook as **Activity 34** in **Student Solutions**	

OR Function

In similar way to the **AND** function, the **OR** function is a **logical** function that provides a result of **true** or **false** based on whether one or more **arguments** are correct.

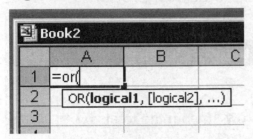

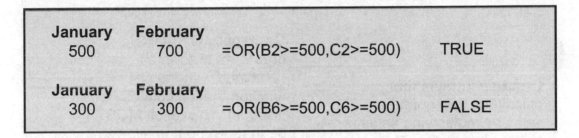

January	February		
500	700	=OR(B2>=500,C2>=500)	TRUE
January	**February**		
300	300	=OR(B6>=500,C6>=500)	FALSE

In the examples above can the function requires either January or February to be equal to or greater than 500 and therefore example one is true and example two is false.

The **OR** function is also very commonly used in conjunction with the **IF** function. Similarly to the **AND** function you can have more than two arguments.

Student Activity 35

This **Activity** is case-sensitive so make sure you use Upper and Lower case where indicated. Carry out the tasks in Column Order.

Column 1		Column 2	
Activity	**Tick**	**Activity**	**Tick**
Go to your Engage account **Open** the **Boat Sales Three** workbook. **Go to** Monthly Sales worksheet Cell D10		**In** row 15 sum the totals by product	
Create a formula that calculates the monthly sales by multiplying sales volume by pricing. This is to be done by customer within product. Give regard to cell referencing		**Go to** cells G10-G13, **create** an IF formula combined with the OR function that calculates discount. The result **MUST** be that discount is allowed if the customer reaches their target volume in boat sales of any type. If discount is not allowed then discounted sales must be equal to total sales. **Copy** to other relevant cells	
Copy this formula to all other relevant cells **In** column F, **create** a formula to sum the total sales by customer		**Go to** cells H10-H13 **Create** a formula using the IF function that shows the statement "Target volume not met" if discount for the customer is zero. The cell should state "Discount allowed" otherwise	
In column F, **create** a formula to sum the total sales by customer		**Save** the workbook as **Activity 35** in **Student Solutions**	

11.4 Date functions

Date functions can be used to insert dates into worksheets so that they are always current or they can be used in formulas to help calculations.

You saw in Session 3 that dates can be formatted in a number of ways and also that a date is a serial number based on a start point of 1st January 1900.

What the functions do:

Function	Result
DATE	A serial number for a particular date
NOW	A serial number for the current date and time
TODAY	A serial number for today's date

Function	Result
DAY	Turns a serial number to a day in a month
MONTH	Turns a serial number into a month
YEAR	Turns a serial number into a year

Examples

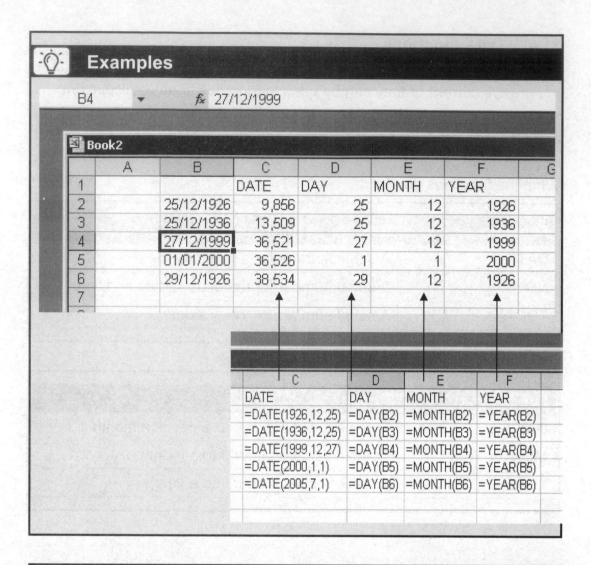

B4	▼	*fx*	27/12/1999

Book2

	A	B	C	D	E	F	G
1			DATE	DAY	MONTH	YEAR	
2		25/12/1926	9,856	25	12	1926	
3		25/12/1936	13,509	25	12	1936	
4		27/12/1999	36,521	27	12	1999	
5		01/01/2000	36,526	1	1	2000	
6		29/12/1926	38,534	29	12	1926	
7							

C	D	E	F
DATE	DAY	MONTH	YEAR
=DATE(1926,12,25)	=DAY(B2)	=MONTH(B2)	=YEAR(B2)
=DATE(1936,12,25)	=DAY(B3)	=MONTH(B3)	=YEAR(B3)
=DATE(1999,12,27)	=DAY(B4)	=MONTH(B4)	=YEAR(B4)
=DATE(2000,1,1)	=DAY(B5)	=MONTH(B5)	=YEAR(B5)
=DATE(2005,7,1)	=DAY(B6)	=MONTH(B6)	=YEAR(B6)

Tip

When you are using Date functions you should format the cell either to a date or number format, dependent upon what you wish to see.

KAPLAN PUBLISHING

Student Activity 36

Column 1	
Activity	**Tick**
Go to your Engage account **Open** the **Contract Labour** workbook. **Go to** sheet 1, cell B2	
In cell B2 **type** =TODAY(), do the same again in cell C2. **In** cell B3 **type** = NOW(), do the same in cell C3 Format cells C2 and C3 to **number – zero decimal places**	
We want to work out our contract labour cost on a rolling basis. We need a start date and then from that we need to calculate the cost on a monthly basis	
In cell C14 **type** =DATE(YEAR($C$7),MONTH($C$7)+**1**,DAY($C$7)) **In** cell D14 **type** =DATE(YEAR(C14),MONTH(C14)+**1**,DAY(C14))	
Now copy the formula in E14 into cells F14 and G14.	
In cell C15 create a formula to subtract C14 from D14 **Copy** the formula into cells D15:F15	
In cell C17 **create** a formula that multiplies the **(days in the period** by **dally production)** by **labour hours per unit**. Give regard to absolute, mixed and relative references **Copy** the formula to cells D17:E17	
In Cell C18 **create** a formula that works out how many contract labourers will be required by dividing **Production hours required** by **Weekly labour hours. Format to zero decimal places** Give regard to absolute, mixed and relative references **Copy** the formula to cells D18:E18	
In Cell 20 **create** a formula that calculates **Contract labour cost** by multiplying **production hours required** by **contract labour rate** Give regard to absolute, mixed and relative references **Copy** the formula to cells D20:E20	
Save the workbook as **Activity 36** in **Student Solutions**	
Now change any of the criteria in cells C7 to C11 and watch what happens to your results	

Tracing errors in formulas

12

Introduction

This chapter will help you to understand the types of errors that can occur and learn how to trace errors in the spreadsheets.

> **KNOWLEDGE**
>
> 3.5 Explain how to find and sort errors in formulas
>
> 3.6 Check spreadsheet information meets needs, using IT tools and making corrections as necessary.

In this session you will learn how to trace errors in formulas and use some of Excel's tools to find and them. In this session you will be looking at:

1. Formula AutoCorrect
2. Error checking
3. Circular references
4. Formula auditing toolbar
5. Trace error

Types of error

You need to be aware of a number of different types of error.

Error	Description
#DIV/0!	This occurs where we have tried to divide by zero or a blank cell.
#N/A	This occurs when data is not available. It is common in LOOKUP functions
#NAME?	This occurs when we use a name that Excel doesn't recognise. This is common in incorrectly spelled function names

#NUM!	This occurs when you place an invalid argument in a function
#REF!	This occurs when a formula uses an invalid cell reference
#VALUE!	This occurs when we attempt to use an incorrect data type

Shortcut

When you are editing a cell that contains a formula, Excel colour codes the formula and then places a coloured border around cells that make up the formula

12.1 Formula AutoCorrect

When writing formulas sometimes parentheses [Brackets] get left out or placed in the wrong order, or you might enter the wrong number of arguments [syntax error]. **Formula AutoCorrect** will pop up on screen and offer to correct the problem. Whilst Excel is very good at finding errors you do need to be careful as it sometimes guesses incorrectly.

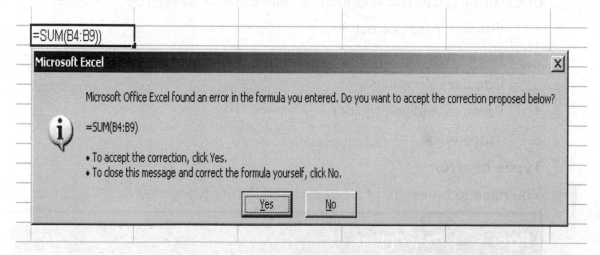

In the example above Excel has correctly determined that one too many parentheses have been placed in the formula. In this instance you can accept the offered solution.

12.2 Error checking

Excel can be set up to check for errors.

EXCEL 2000	EXCEL 2003	EXCEL 2007
/Tools/	/Tools/	/Windows icon/
/Options/	/Options/	/Excel Options/
/Error Checking/	/Error Checking/	/Formulas/
		/Error Checking/

This option allows you to set your own rules for error checking. It is probably best left in its default setting.

Excel also has a more local error checking tool. When you enter a formula Excel will place a flag in a cell if it thinks you are making an error.

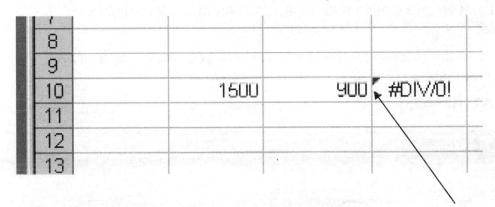

In the above example Excel has put a flag in the cell where it thinks there is an error. If you click into the error cell you will be given the option to review and deal with the error.

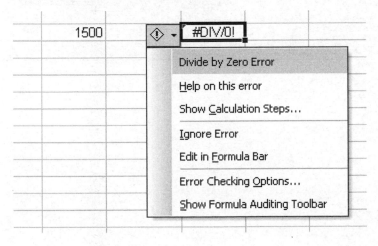

Above you can see a **Divide by zero error**. You now have the opportunity to get help from a number of sources, or ignore the error.

- If you click Help on this error the Excel Help system will pop up and you can ask questions and seek help from here

- Show calculation steps is dealt with later in the session

- You can choose to ignore the error. This is OK if you know what the problem is and can fix it, but you should not simply ignore the error as you will create problems elsewhere.

- Edit in formula bar puts the cursor in the formula bar, and you can fix your problem

- Error checking options will activate the Error Checking dialogue box mentioned above.

- Show Formula Auditing Toolbar is dealt with later in this session

12.3 Circular References

A circular reference is a common error and occurs when you try to include the cell that we are writing a formula in as part of the formula. For example:

If you typed the following formula into Cell A3, you would get a circular reference message.

=sum(A1+A2+A3)

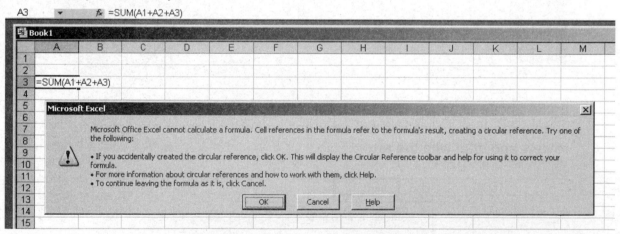

KAPLAN PUBLISHING

We have a number of options to resolve the problem:

Excel 2003	Excel 2007
• OK, will present the Circular reference toolbar [below] and the Help facility	• OK, will present the Help facility
• Cancel, leaves the error in the formula. You should only do this if you want the circular reference. It is possible to want to do this, but, it is beyond this syllabus, therefore, don't do it.	• Cancel, leaves the error in the formula. You should only do this if you want the circular reference. It is possible to want to do this, but, it is beyond this syllabus, therefore, don't do it.
• Help, this will bring up the Help facility	• Error Checking on Formula Tab is available for fixing the problem

The **Circular Reference** toolbar or **Error Checking** are tools designed to aid in solving the circular reference.

Click into the cell that contains the circular reference and it will allow you to use:

- Trace Dependents, these are formulas that depend on this solution for their data

- Trace Precedents, these are cells or formulas that precede [come before] the cell with the circular reference

The example above has no Dependents and therefore another example has been written to show these. Note the way that Excel has placed blue arrows showing precedents and dependents.

Tip
If Excel does not give the Circular Reference Toolbar automatically
Excel 2000/2003 Select   View/ Toolbars/ Circular Reference
Excel 2007 Select   Formulas tab

12.4   Formula Auditing Toolbar

The **Formula Auditing Toolbar/Tab** is a very useful tool for finding and controlling errors in spreadsheets – especially complex ones

EXCEL 2000	EXCEL 2003	EXCEL 2007
/Tools/ /Formula Auditing/ /Show Formula Auditing Toolbar/	/Tools/ /Formula Auditing/ /Show Formula Auditing Toolbar/	/Formulas Tab/

Button	Explanation
Error Checking.	Where an error such as #DIV/0! Occurs Excel will describe what the error is and offer help on fixing it
Trace Dependents	as earlier
Remove Trace Dependents arrows	
Trace Precedents	as earlier
Remove Trace Precedents arrows	

Remove all arrows	
Trace Error	see next section
New comment	Allows comments to be written about cells.
Circle Invalid data	covered in a later session
Clear validation circles	covered in a later session
Show Watch Window	a useful tool to watch the value in a particular cell[s]
Evaluate Formula	A very useful tool for evaluating each part of a formula. Can be used to drill down into formulas to check what they are doing

12.5   Trace Error

In more complex spreadsheets where an error occurs it is often the case that what causes the error can be elsewhere in the worksheet, workbook or even another workbook. For **Trace Error** to work the active cell must be the one with the error in it.

- **Trace Error** - when activated - inserts an arrow showing where the error is coming from when the error is in the same worksheet.

- **Trace Error** when activated will insert a dashed line with an icon of a worksheet when the error is in another worksheet or workbook

- The formula bar provides the path to the other workbook. Especially useful if the workbook that contains the error is closed

KAPLAN PUBLISHING

Charts and graphs

13

Introduction

This chapter will guide you how to create a number of different graphs and how to move and change these charts and graphs in the spreadsheet

KNOWLEDGE
3.3 Select and use appropriate tools and techniques to generate, develop and format charts and graphs.

In this session we will be examining Charts and Graphs. We will be looking at several types and their construction, formatting and location.

In essence there is very little difference between a chart and a graph and the term is interchangeable. One minor difference is that some charts do not have axes, whilst graphs always do.

13.1 Chart and Graph Terminology

Listed below are the more common charting terms

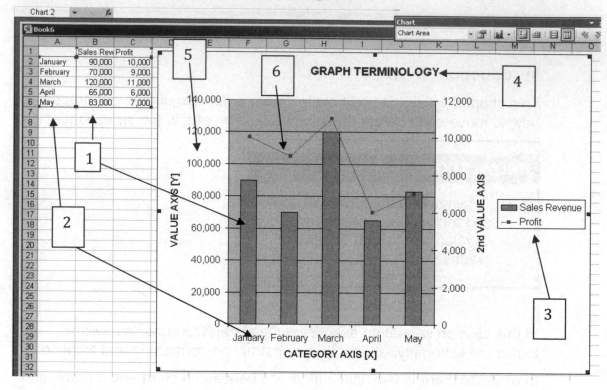

1. **Data Series**. These are the numbers **[values]** from which Excel is creating the graph. These are plotted on the **Value or 'Y' axis**.

2. **Category**. The information that identifies the data series. This is plotted along the **Category or 'X' axis**.

3. **Legend**. These identify the different types of data series and can have a number of keys to identify particular series

4. **Title**. Gives meaning to the graph.

5. **Scale**. Both the 'X' and the 'Y' axis can have a scale. These identify the range of values in the data series.

6. **Data Point**. This denotes the value of a particular data series. **Data Labels** can be placed next to data points to give greater meaning. Data Points have Data Markers. Data Markers are different shapes and colours for each data series

13.2 Creating Charts and Graphs

Within Excel there are two basic ways to display charts and graphs. There is no right or wrong way it is user preference. It is also a simple matter to switch between the two types.

1. **Chart Sheet**, here the chart or graph becomes the entire worksheet.

2. **Embedded**, here the chart or graph is located on the sheet that contains the data. The chart can be moved around to suit the user.

In Excel there are three ways in which a graph or chart can be created.

Highlight the data you want in your chart and press F11. Excel will create a default [column] chart on a chart sheet.

Open the chart toolbar. /View/ Toolbars/ Chart/. Then select the graph type that you want. [Note that for Excel 2007 this is done via the Insert tab].

Use the chart wizard. /Insert/ Chart/ or click the graph icon on the toolbar. [Note that for Excel 2007 this is done via the Insert tab and chart tools].

13.3 Types of Charts and Graphs

You need to be aware of the following types of graph

*   Bar and Column charts
*   Pie and Doughnut charts
*   Scatter graph
*   Bubble chart
*   Single and Double line graphs
*   Multiple graph types on one chart

When it comes to choosing the correct type of chart to use there are no hard and fast rules. It is generally up to the report writer to choose, and, as you are trying to show graphically what a series of numbers represent it is sometimes best to play around until the best option is found. Within each type of graph or chart you will find sub-types of the same graph with a mini-explanation of each, plus you get a preview of what your graph will look like.

Bar and Column Charts

These are effectively the same idea with the bars and columns representing data points and the height of the column or length of the bar representing a value.

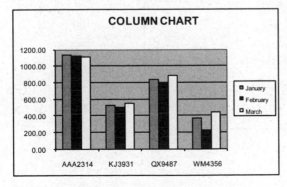
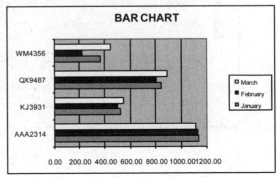

Pie and Doughnut Charts

Pie and Doughnut charts are also very similar. They both represent proportions of a whole [example: percentage of males over 25] and neither of them have axes. The major difference between the two is that a Pie Chart can only have one data series whilst a doughnut can have two or more. These types of charts are most effective with a small number of data points – otherwise the chart becomes too busy and crowded.

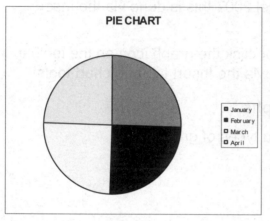
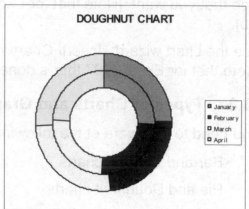

Scatter graph (XY)

This type of graph has two **value** axes and no category axis, and is typically used to show the relationship of two sets of numbers. In the example below the relationship is of sales volume to sales revenue. The data points [represented by diamonds] show the intersection of the two sets of numbers

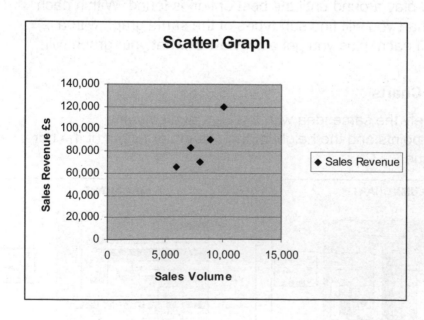

Bubble Chart

A bubble chart is very similar to a scatter graph in that it compares values. The difference here is that a third data series is added. The third data series is represented by the size of the bubble. In our example below the bubble represents profit.

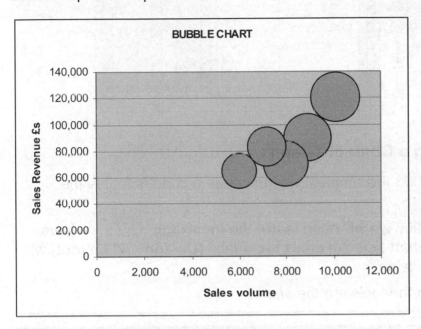

Single and Double Line Graphs

Line charts are used to plot continuous data and are very useful for showing trends. The more **data series** there are the more lines you can have on your graph.

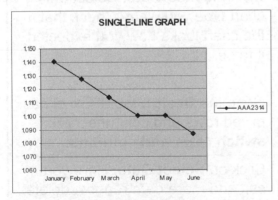

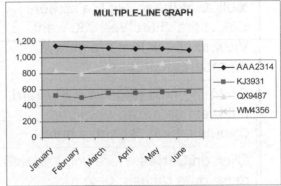

Multiple graph types on one chart

Also known as **Combination Charts** these charts must consist of at least two data series. With this chart type you can have either two graph types on **one** axis or insert a second **value** or 'Y' axis.

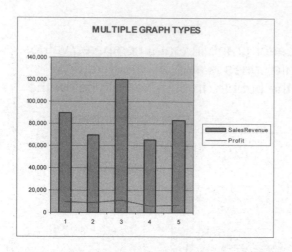

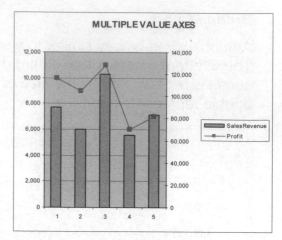

13.4 Creating a Chart or Graph

• For Excel 2003 the simplest way to create a chart is to use the **wizard**.

• For Excel 2007 we will need to use the **insert tab**. Once we have selected a chart type the **chart tools** tabs **[Design** and **Layout]** will become available.

For either version the tools are the same.

EXCEL 2003	EXCEL 2007
Highlight the data you wish to include in the chart	Highlight the data you wish to include in the chart
Start the **chart wizard** from the toolbar at the top of the screen. Select the chart type you want. View to check that the data is represented properly	Click the **insert tab**. Select the chart type you want. Check that the chart looks how you expected it to be
Go to the next page of the wizard. If Excel has mixed rows and columns, then change it here	Go to the **Design** tab. If Excel has mixed rows and columns, click **switch rows and columns**.
Click on **Series**. Here you can add more data ranges, delete unwanted ranges or alter existing ranges. If you haven't already done it you can add **Category [X] axis labels**	Click on **Select Data**. Here you can add more data ranges, delete unwanted ranges or alter existing ranges. If you haven't already done it you can add **Category [X] axis labels**

Go to the next page of the **wizard**	Go to the **Layout tab**
• Add a **chart title** and **X** and **Y axis** labels	• Add a **chart title** and **X** and **Y axis** labels
• Go to **Axes** and decide if you want axes or not	• Go to **Axes** and decide if you want axes or not
• Go to **Gridlines** and decide if you want gridlines or not	• Go to **Gridlines** and decide if you want gridlines or not
• Go to **Legend** and decide if you want a legend and where you want to place it	• Go to **Legend** and decide if you want a legend and where you want to place it
• Go to **Data labels** and decide if you want them, and if you need a separator	• Go to **Data Labels** and decide if you want them and where
• Go to **Data Tables** and decide if you want a data table and whether you want a **legend key** alongside of it.	• Go to **Data Tables** and decide if you want a data table and whether you want a **legend key** alongside of it.
• Go to the last page of the wizard and decide whether you want the chart **embedded** or as a **chart sheet**.	• Go to the **Designs** tab, click the **Move Chart** icon and decide if you want the chart **embedded** or as a **chart sheet**.

13.5   Making Changes to your chart

It is easy to make changes to you chart. You can:

- Click on the edge of the chart and then use the wizard / chart tools to make your changes.

- Alternatively you can **Right-Click** on the part of the chart that you want to change. You will be presented with a drop down menu.

Some changes that you can make:

- Add a **Trend-line**. Right click on a **data-series** on your chart and click add trendline.

- Adding a **Secondary** value axis. Right click on the **data-series** you want the secondary axis for. Click **format data-series** and click secondary axis.

- Add a <u>**Data-Series**</u>. Right click the centre of the chart and click **source data [2003]** or **select data [2007]**. Click **Add**, then add a series name and series values.

- Adding second graph/chart type. Right click the **data-series** you wish to change and click **chart type [2003] / change series chart type [2007]**. Select your chart type.

- You can add text to a chart by adding a text box and then typing into it.

  - **Excel 2003**, Insert / Toolbars/ Drawing Toolbar
  - **Excel 2007**, Insert Tab or Chart Tools / Layout Tab

 Student Activity 37

This **Activity** is case-sensitive so make sure you use Upper and Lower case where indicated. Carry out the tasks in Column Order.

Column 1		Column 2	
Activity	**Tick**	**Activity**	**Tick**
Go to your engage account **Open** the **Graph Sales Data** workbook. **Go to** Sheet 1		Move the chart to the right of **Quarter 4 Forecast**.	
Highlight Cells B13-E16		Resize the chart to fit on screen and leave all data showing.	
Embed a **Column Chart** in Sheet 1			
Chart Title is **Quarterly Sales 20X0** No Category **X** title Category **Y** Title is £000's Delete the **Legend** Show the **Data Table** with **Legend**		**Save** the workbook as **Activity 37** in **Student Solutions**	

Student Activity 38

This **Activity** is case-sensitive so make sure you use Upper and Lower case where indicated. Carry out the tasks in Column Order.

Column 1		Column 2	
Activity	**Tick**	**Activity**	**Tick**
Go to Student Solutions **Open** the **Activity 37** workbook. **Go to** Sheet 1		**Remove** the **Data Table**	
Copy the embedded chart and **paste** it to Sheet 3		**Change** the figure in Cell A2 and note the changes to the graph	
Change the chart **location** to a **Chart Sheet**			
Add the **Quarter 4** data-series to the chart		**Save** the workbook as **Activity 38**	

 Student Activity 39

This **Activity** is case-sensitive so make sure you use Upper and Lower case where indicated. Carry out the tasks in Column Order.

Column 1		Column 2	
Activity	**Tick**	**Activity**	**Tick**
Go to Engage **Open** the **Graph Sales Data** workbook. **Go to** Sheet 2		**Select** the **Gross Profit** data series on the chart and **format** it so that the **weight** of the line increases in thickness	
Select the **Gross Profit** data series on the chart and **change** it so that it is a **Line Graph** chart type		**Select** the **Gross Profit** data series on the chart and **add** a **linear** trendline to the chart. Change the trendline colour to **Bright Green**	
Select the **Gross Profit** data series on the chart and **format** it so that it has a **secondary value axis**		**Save** the workbook as **Activity 39** in **Student Solutions**	

Data validation

Introduction

This chapter will explain how to restrict data within cells and give a brief introduction to named ranges.

KNOWLEDGE
1.1 Identify what numerical and other information is needed in the spreadsheet and how it should be structured.

Within Excel there is a tool that allows the writer of the spreadsheet to determine what type of data is entered into a cell or cells.

EXCEL 2000	EXCEL 2003	EXCEL 2007
/Data/ /Validation/	/Data/ /Validation/	/Data Tab/ /Data Validation/ /Data Validation/

When you decide a cell should be validated you will be faced with the following dialogue box.

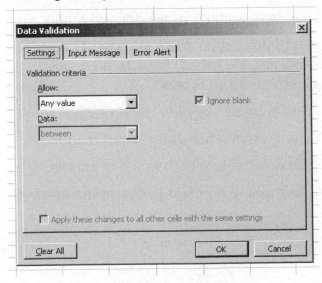

There are three tabs to understand:

1. **Settings**: allows you to determine what type of data will be displayed in the cell

2. **Input message:** allows you to write a message that will appear when the user tries to enter data into the cell

3. **Error Alert:** allows you to write a message that will appear if the user tries to enter invalid data.

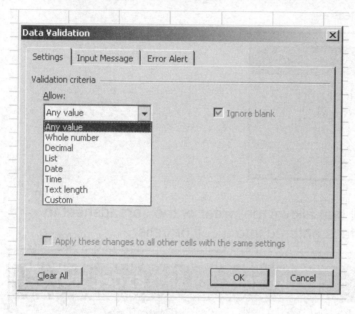

From the **settings** tab we can select the data type we will allow.

1. **Any value:** allows any value to be entered

2. **Whole number:** allows only whole numbers to be entered into the cell. The writer can determine a range that can be used.

3. **Decimal:** allows decimal numbers within a writer defined range

4. **List:** allows the user to select from a drop down list only. The writer will need to determine the list, and the list will have to be on the same worksheet unless a **named range** is used.

5. **Date:** allows dates to be used within a pre-determined range

6. **Time:** allows times to be used within a pre-determined range

7. **Text length:** allows ext to be entered to a certain set of criteria

8. **Custom:** Allows a **logical formula** to be used to determine what will be allowed in the cell

Validation circles

EXCEL 2000	EXCEL 2003	EXCEL 2007
/Tools/	/Tools/	/Data Tab/
/Formula Auditing/	/Formula Auditing/	/Data Validation/
/Show formula auditing toolbar/	/Show formula auditing toolbar/	/Circle invalid data
/Circle invalid data/	/Circle invalid data/	

Where a spreadsheet has been previously populated with data and then validation is applied it is likely that some data could be wrong. There is a tool known as validation circles that will highlight these errors

Student Activity 40

This **Activity** is case-sensitive so make sure you use Upper and Lower case where indicated. Carry out the tasks in Column Order.

Column 1		Column 2	
Activity	Tick	Activity	Tick
Open a blank workbook Go to Sheet 1		In the Name Box type DropDownList then Enter Key	
Go to Cell A1, Type John Go to Cell A2, Type Joan Go to Cell A3, Type Jonty		Go to Sheet 2, Cell D5 Go to Data Validation Select allow from List. In Source type =DropDownList Check out the result, try and type Fred into cell D5	
Highlight cells A1-A3		Save the workbook as Activity 40 in Student Solutions on your pc	

Student Activity 41

Column 1	
Activity	**Tick**
Go to your Kaplan Engage account **Open** the **Product Order** workbook. **Go to** Products, **Highlight** Cells A2-A21 and create a **Named Range** ProductCode	
Go to the **Order Sheet** worksheet. In Cell A12 **create** Data Validation to pick up the product code from a drop down list using the named range. Copy and paste-special the validation down to row 40	
In Cell B12 **create** a VLOOKUP formula that looks up the product code in Cell $A12, uses the range $A$1-$D$21 from the products worksheet and returns the 2nd column, copy this formula to row 40 Use an **IF** statement to stop the #N/A error appearing	
In Cell C12 **create** Data Validation that checks that the order quantity meets the minimum requirement. You should create an **IF** statement that checks the minimum order quantity in Cell B1 and returns an error message if **false** =IF(C12>=$B$1,TRUE,FALSE) **Create** a Data Validation input message that has the title **Minimum Order Quantity** and carries the message Please ensure that your order quantity is greater than the minimum **Create** a Data Validation **STOP** message that has the title **Minimum Order Quantity** and carries the message Your order is not large enough, check and try again.	
Enter a formula in Cell E8 that always shows Today's date **Set** the Print Area from Cell A7-E48	
Enter some product codes in column A from the drop down list and enter some order quantities to see what happens.	
Check the order on print preview	
Save the workbook as **Activity 41** in **Student Solutions**	

Spreadsheet templates

15

Introduction

This chapter will help you to understand what a template does and where to store it, and how to retrieve it.

KNOWLEDGE

1.4 Store and retrieve spreadsheet files effectively, in line with company guidelines and conventions where applicable.

Templates are useful tools for creating and storing workbooks that are used constantly. The most used templates are the Excel workbooks that contain three sheets that we use all the time. There are also a number of templates readily available in Excel.

It is simple enough job to create our own template. When you do this you should save it to a special template folder. When you do Excel will add an **.xlt** or **.xltx** extension to the workbook.

The next time you want to open the template, you open it from the temp folder and Excel will create the new workbook with the same name as the template – but it will add a number to it.

Student Activity 42

This **Activity** is case-sensitive so make sure you use Upper and Lower case where indicated. Carry out the tasks in Column Order. Solutions to all activities are found in your Kaplan Engage online account.

Column 1		Column 2	
Activity	Tick	Activity	Tick
Open **Activity 41**		**Open** the template up again from Templates/ On my computer [Excel 2003] My Templates [Excel 2007]	
Save as **Save as Type** Save the file as **Product Order Temp** Save the file as a template in the **Default Template Location**		**Create** a new workbook from **Product Order Temp** Note the name the Excel gives the worksheet	
Close the template		**Note** unless the template is saved in a special folder labelled by Excel it will not open as a new workbook next time you load it. It will open as a template.	
Click File/New [Excel 2003] **Click** Windows Icon/New [Excel 2007]		**Save** the workbook as **Activity 42 Temp** as a template in **Student Solutions**	

Spreadsheet protection

16

Introduction

This chapter will show you how to protect your spreadsheets so that no other user can change the content of the spreadsheet.

KNOWLEDGE

1.4 Store and retrieve spreadsheet files effectively, in line with company guidelines and conventions where applicable.

In this session you will learn how to:

- Hide Rows and Columns
- How to hide formulae
- How to lock cells
- How to protect a worksheet
- How to protect a workbook

16.1 How to hide rows and columns

EXCEL 2000	EXCEL 2003	EXCEL 2007
/Highlight the area around the hidden row or column /Format/ /Column, Row or Sheet/ /Hide or Unhide/	/Highlight the area around the hidden row or column /Format/ /Column, Row or Sheet/ /Hide or Unhide/	/Home tab/ /Format/ /Hide or Unhide/ /Column, Row or Sheet

The simplest way to hide rows and columns is to highlight the rows and columns you want to hide, **right –click** and then click **hide** in the menu.

To unhide the columns or rows you should **highlight** either side if the hidden row or column and then **right-click** and click **unhide** from the menu.

If you hide column **A** you will need to carry out the routine in the table above.

The only way to hide a worksheet is via the table above.

16.2 How to hide formulas

To hide formulas you will need to go to the Format Cells dialogue box, open the protection tab and click **hidden**. It must be stressed that the formulas will only become hidden when the worksheet is protected

16.3 How to protect cells

Protecting cells means that you cannot enter data into the cell

All cells are automatically protected as soon as you protect a worksheet. There will be instances when you have a protected worksheet where you do not want some cells protected. To do this you need to bring up the format dialogue box and un-tick the **locked** radio button.

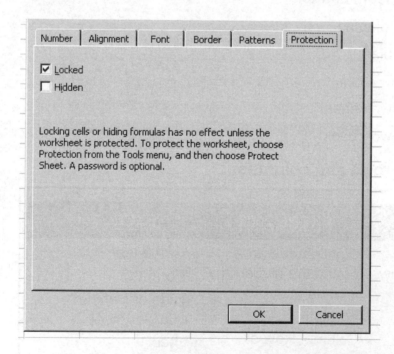

16.4 How to protect a worksheet

EXCEL 2000	EXCEL 2003	EXCEL 2007
/Tools/	/Tools/	/Review Tab/
/Protection/	/Protection/	/Protect Worksheet/
/Protect Sheet/	/Protect Sheet/	

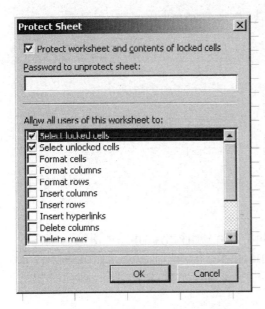

Opening the Protect Sheet dialogue box allows the writer to protect locked cells, hide formulas and to add a password to protect a sheet [optional].

In addition the writer can allow users to carry out certain actions. [Tick to allow]

Note

If you password protect a worksheet and then forget the password you will not be able to open the sheet.

16.5 How to protect a workbook

File-Saving Options

EXCEL 2000	EXCEL 2003	EXCEL 2007
/File/	/File/	/Windows Icon/
/Save-as/	/Save-as/	/Save-as/
/Tools/	/Tools/	/Tools/
/General Options/	/General Options/	/General Options/

When you save a workbook in the **Save as** mode you get the option to set a password to both open and modify the sheet. If you set the **password to open** the worksheet the user will not be able to **read-only**. If you forget the password you will not be able to gain access to the worksheet.

Workbook Protection

EXCEL 2000	EXCEL 2003	EXCEL 2007
/Tools/ /Protection/ /Protect Workbook/	/Tools/ /Protection/ /Protect Workbook/	/Review Tab/ /Protect Worksheet/ /Protect structure and windows/

The writer is also able to protect the workbook from changes as well

You can prevent users from adding or deleting worksheets, or displaying hidden worksheets. You can also prevent users from changing the sizes or positions of the windows you set up to display a workbook. This protection applies to the entire workbook.

Student Activity 43

This **Activity** is case-sensitive so make sure you use Upper and Lower case where indicated. Carry out the tasks in Column Order. All solutions are online in your Kaplan Engage account.

Column 1		Column 2	
Activity	**Tick**	**Activity**	**Tick**
Open **Activity 36** from the folder on your pc		**Go to** the Protection tab and tick **Hidden**, then close the dialogue box	
Highlight cells C7-C11		**Go to** Tools / Protection [2003] Review Tab [2007]	
Right Click Format Cells		**Click** Protect Sheet, allow the user to only select **Unlocked Cells** and **Format Cells**	
Open the **Format Cells** dialogue box		Close the dialogue box without setting a password	
Go to the **Protection** tab		**Format** Cells C7-C11 with a bright yellow fill and make the text dark blue and **Bold**	
Untick Locked, close the dialogue box		Try moving around the sheet, and change some data in cells C7-C11, observe the results	
Highlight the entire sheet, and reopen the **Format Cells** dialogue box		**Save** the workbook as **Activity 43** in **Student Solutions**	

Sharing workbooks

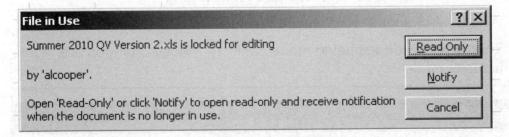

Introduction

This chapter will show you the function of 'read only' and how to share workbooks

KNOWLEDGE

1.4 Store and retrieve spreadsheet files effectively, in line with company guidelines and conventions where applicable.

Normally when a user tries to open a workbook that is in use already they are presented with the dialogue box below. Here they have three options.

1. They could open the file **Read-Only**. They can have access to the file, but they can only save changes they make if they use **Save-as** and give the file a new name.

2. They could open the file with the **Notify** button. Here they can view the file and when presented with another dialogue box informing them that the file is available for **read-write** they can make their changes.

3. They can click **Cancel** to close the dialogue box without opening the file.

File in Use   ? X

Summer 2010 QV Version 2.xls is locked for editing   Read Only

by 'alcooper'.   Notify

Open 'Read-Only' or click 'Notify' to open read-only and receive notification when the document is no longer in use.   Cancel

Excel cannot be considered a multi-user application. It does, however, have a feature called **Share Workbook** that does allow more than one user on a **network** to update a spreadsheet at the same time.

EXCEL 2000	EXCEL 2003	EXCEL 2007
/Tools/ /Share Workbook/	/Tools/ /Share Workbook/	/Review Tab/ /Share Workbook/

If the writer follows the path above they will be presented with the following dialogue box. If they tick the **Allow Changes** box the workbook will allow multiple users. When in this mode Excel keeps a track of the changes that have been made. Also the 2nd tab becomes available.

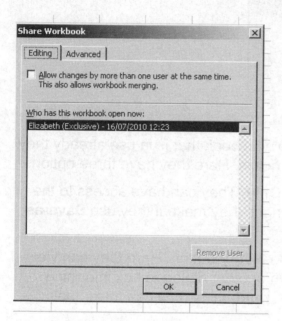
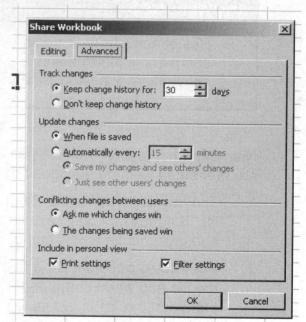

The writer can then stipulate:

- If changes should be recorded and for how long
- When the changes will come into effect
- That, when changes being made conflict – whose changes are actually made.

Note

When a workbook is shared most of the functionality of the spreadsheet is impaired. For instance: deleting; merging, insert charts and objects, conditional formats, data validation and subtotals. To name but a few.

Consolidating worksheets

18

Introduction

This chapter will show you how to join one or more workbooks together using the consolidation tool and to understand the various aspects of this function.

KNOWLEDGE
2.3   Select and use a range of tools and techniques to analyse and interpret data to meet requirements.

We have seen previously how to join two or more worksheets/ workbooks together to consolidate the information in these objects into one place. Excel comes equipped with a **Consolidation** tool to aid us in this task

EXCEL 2000	EXCEL 2003	EXCEL 2007
/Data/ /Consolidate/	/Data/ /Consolidate/	/Data tab/ /Consolidate/

There are five matters that need to be considered before the consolidation takes place:

1. If you consolidate without creating links to the source data, the tool will consolidate using the function you choose. However, if the source data changes the consolidation will not.

2. Consolidating by creating links to the source data. Here, if the source data changes then the consolidation updates also.

3. The source data does not need to be open to be consolidated, but it is easier to do.

4. You can use row and column labels to aid in the consolidation but you are only able to do this if the consolidation is using categories. This is very effective as the row and column labels do not need to be in the same position in the worksheets. However, the row and column labels **MUST** be spelt exactly the same. [They are not affected by upper and lower case]

5. If the construction of the worksheets in all the source data is the same you can consolidate by using just the position of the data in the worksheet.

The **Consolidation Tool** when opened presents you with the following dialogue box.

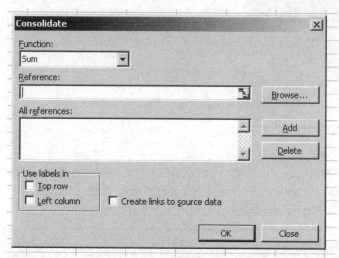

When you have linked to some source data [Reference] this should be added to the list of **All References**.

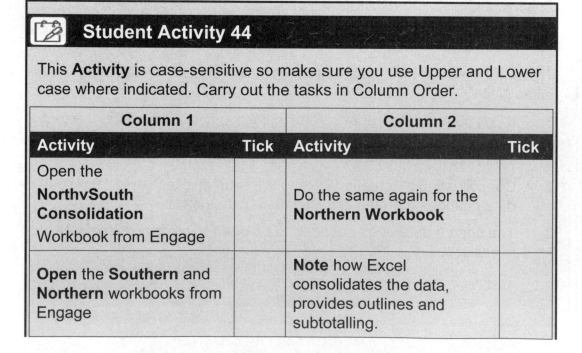

Student Activity 44

This **Activity** is case-sensitive so make sure you use Upper and Lower case where indicated. Carry out the tasks in Column Order.

Column 1		Column 2	
Activity	**Tick**	**Activity**	**Tick**
Open the **NorthvSouth Consolidation** Workbook from Engage		Do the same again for the **Northern Workbook**	
Open the **Southern** and **Northern** workbooks from Engage		**Note** how Excel consolidates the data, provides outlines and subtotalling.	

Go to the NorthvSouth Consolidation, **District Totals** worksheet, Cell B2		
Open the consolidation tool, and using the Sum Function and Links to the source data **Reference** to the **Southern Workbook** CellsB2-M5	**Save** the workbook as **Activity 44** in **Student Solutions** in the folder on your pc	

 Student Activity 45

This **Activity** is case-sensitive so make sure you use Upper and Lower case where indicated. Carry out the tasks in Column Order.

Column 1		Column 2	
Activity	Tick	**Activity**	Tick
Open the **EastvWest Consolidation** workbook		Do the same again for the **Western Workbook**	
Open the **Eastern** and **Western** workbooks		**Note** how Excel consolidates the data, provides outlines and subtotalling.	
Go to the EastvWest Consolidation, **District Totals** worksheet, Cell A1		**Note** how Excel has correctly added up the product codes and months even though they are not in the same order	
Open the consolidation tool, and using • the Sum Function • and Links to the source data • and using labels in Top Row and Left Column **Reference** to the **Eastern Workbook** Cells A1-M13		**Save** the workbook as **Activity 45** in **Student Solutions**	

Creating simple pivot tables

19

Introduction

This chapter will show you how to use the function of pivot tables as a form of consolidation, how to insert formulas into these pivot tables, and how to create charts from pivot tables.

KNOWLEDGE

2.3   Select and use a range of tools and techniques to analyse and interpret data to meet requirements.

3.3   Select and use appropriate tools and techniques to generate, develop and format charts and graphs.

In this session we will be covering:

- Construction of Pivot Tables
- Pivot Table tools
  - (i)   Formatting
  - (ii)   Grand Totals and Sub-totals
  - (iii)   Grouping and Ungrouping
  - (iv)   Refreshing data
  - (v)   Changing the calculation function
  - (vi)   Adding Formulas to Pivot Tables
- Pivot Charts

19.1   Construction of Pivot Tables

A **Pivot Table** is a tool used for turning tables of data into meaningful reports. The tool can be used to create reports from external sources, multiple-workbooks [another consolidation tool] and workbooks. *For this syllabus we will be creating Pivot Tables from workbooks.*

The syllabus requires that we are able to create simple Pivot Tables and we will therefore not be using all the functions that are available. We will, however, be creating charts from pivot table reports.

In essence a Pivot Table is a means of taking raw data and presenting it so that the user can understand what they are looking at. When the Pivot Table is initiated a cross-tabulation of the data will be created. To create a Pivot Table:

EXCEL 2000	EXCEL 2003	EXCEL 2007
/Data/ /Pivot Table and Pivot Chart Report/	/Data/ /Pivot Table and Pivot Chart Report/	/Insert tab/ /Pivot Table/

When you follow the path above you will be presented with a **'Wizard'** designed to guide you through the steps in creating the Pivot Table. You will find it easier to create the Pivot Table if you highlight the data you want to include in the table, this will avoid the need to choose it later.

At this stage you get to choose whether you want a Pivot Table or Pivot Chart. It is just as easy to create a chart once the Pivot Table is created so you will learn to create charts from within the Pivot Table.

You will be asked where your data range is. If it has been selected previously this will be indicated in the dialogue box. If the data range hasn't already been selected it can be done now by either typing in the range or **Pointing** to it.

You will also be asked where the Pivot Table is to be located: either in the worksheet; or in a new worksheet

Once the Pivot Table has been created you will be faced with the following dialogue box.

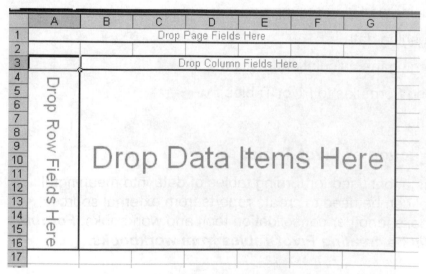

A **Pivot Table Field List** will also be presented. You will drag and drop fields from the list into the table. If at any time the Field List is not in view, simply click into the Pivot and it will appear

There are four parts to the Pivot Table:

1. **Page Fields**. This area is used to choose items that will create different views of the data. For instance it could be that you want to create a report that could show the data by looking at different sales-persons.

2. **Column Fields**. Here you drag and drop one or more fields that will form the columns of the table.

3. **Row Fields**. Here you drag and drop one or more fields that will form the rows of the table.

4. **Data Items**. Here you drag and drop a field – or possibly more than one – that you want to analyse. It is usual for this to be a numeric field, although it is not necessary. If you drop a numeric field the default is for this to be summed – this can be changed later. If the field is not numeric the default is for this to be counted.

19.2 Pivot Table Tools

A Pivot Table is a very powerful tool and there are many things that can be done to enhance it. Below are listed some of them

(i) **Formatting**

Most of the formatting tools available to spreadsheets are also available to Pivot Tables

Auto-Format

There are a number of auto-formats that can be used to enhance the Pivot Table:

- **Excel 2003**. Format / Auto-Format

- **Excel 2007**. Design Tab

(ii) **Adding and Removing Grand Totals and Sub Totals**

Grand Totals

- **Excel 2003**. Right Click anywhere in the Pivot Table

  - Table Options / Either **tick** or **un-tick** grand totals for rows and/or columns

- **Excel 2007**. Right Click anywhere in the Pivot Table

  - Pivot Table Options / Totals and Filters / Either **tick** or **un-tick** grand totals for rows and/or columns

Sub-Totals

- **Excel 2003.** Right Click anywhere in the **Column Field** that you wish to sub-total

    – Field Settings / Subtotals / Choose option

- **Excel 2007**. Right Click anywhere in the **Column Field** that you wish to sub-total

    – Field Settings / Subtotals & Filters / Choose option

(iii) **Grouping and Ungrouping Column and Row Fields**

Sometimes it is appropriate to **Group** together certain fields. For example where you have **Month Fields** you may wish to group them into quarters.

- **Excel 2003**. Highlight what you wish to group. Right Click anywhere in the **Column Field** or **Row Field** that you wish to sub-total.

    – Group and show detail / Group or Ungroup

- **Excel 2007.** Highlight what you wish to group. Right Click anywhere in the **Column Field** or **Row Field** that you wish to sub-total.

    – Group or Ungroup

(iv) **Refreshing data**

A Pivot Table will not update automatically. Therefore, if you add, change or delete data you will need to refresh the table.

- **Right-click**. Refresh

(v) **Changing the calculation function**

Pivot Tables usually default to **sum** for numeric data and **count** for non-numeric data. This may not be what you want and it is easy to change.

Go to the top left hand cell of the row and columns and you will find the calculation function, in the example below **Sum of Quantity** [Cell A3].

	A	B	C
1	Month	(All) ▼	
2			
3	Sum of Quantity	Product Code ▼	
4	Salesperson ▼	AAA2314	KJ3931
5	Eva Nasri	1155	1∠
6	James Beardsley	963	1:
7	Grand Total	2118	2ɛ
8			

- **Excel 2003**. Right-click on the function / Field settings / Choose a new option.

- **Excel 2007**. Right-click on the function / Value Field settings / Choose a new option.

(vi) **Adding Formulas to Pivot Tables**

You cannot change the data in the **data items** in a Pivot Table. However, you can insert formulas into certain parts of the Pivot Table. These formulas are not constructed in the formula bar, they are constructed in a special dialogue box. There are two types of formulas that you can write:

1. **Calculated Item:** This can only be created in a **page, row** or **column** field. It cannot happen in the **data area**. This calculation uses item[s] within a particular field to create a new item for that field. For example you may be analysing data by months, by inserting a calculated item you could create a **quarter field** in a way similar to grouping.

2. **Calculated Field:** This can only be created for the **data area** of the table. It cannot happen in the page, row or column fields. Here the calculation would involve creating new data from existing data. For instance we could add a percentage to a sales revenue figure or, calculate the average sales price per unit sold.

Student Activity 46

This **Activity** is case-sensitive so make sure you use Upper and Lower case where indicated. Carry out the tasks in Column Order. Solutions to all activities can be found in your Kaplan Engage account.

Column 1		Column 2	
Activity	**Tick**	**Activity**	**Tick**
Open the **ResultsPivotData** Workbook from Engage		**Whilst in Table Options** tick 'for error values' 'for empty cells'	
Go to DataSheet and **highlight** Cells A1-E187		**Insert** a **calculated item** into the column area. Call this **Pass %** **Create** a formula that divides pass by total who took exam. **= Pass/(Fail+Pass)** **Add** this to the items.	
Create a **Pivot Table** in a new worksheet		Return to the Pivot Table, format Pass % as a percentage to 0 decimal places.	
Page Field = Teacher **Row Field** = Exam **Column Field** = Result **Data Items** = Name		Go to **Page Area** and toggle between different teachers, note the effect	
Go to Table Options and **remove** Grand Totals for rows and columns		**Save** the workbook as **Activity 46** in **Student Solutions** on your pc	

Student Activity 47

This **Activity** is case-sensitive so make sure you use Upper and Lower case where indicated. Carry out the tasks in Column Order.

Column 1		Column 2	
Activity	**Tick**	**Activity**	**Tick**
Open the **ResultsPivotData** Workbook from Engage again		**Go to** the Row Area and **highlight** the cells called Geography, History and Sport **Group** these items and call the group **Sundry**	
Go to DataSheet and **highlight** Cells A1-E187		**Drag and Drop** the new field [Exam2] to the Page Area	
Create a **Pivot Table** in a new worksheet		**Drag and Drop** the **Result** field to the right of the **Exam** field in the **Row Area**	
Page Field – Result **Row Field** = Exam **Column Field** = Teacher **Data Items** = Name		**Format** the results as number with 0 decimal places	
Go to the Row Area and **highlight** the cells called English, Maths and Science **Group** these items and call the group **Core**		**Toggle** between Core and Sundry in the **Page** area	
		Save the workbook as **Activity 47** in **Student Solutions**	

19.3 Pivot Charts

Once you have created your Pivot Table it is very easy to create a chart. By clicking the **Pivot Chart** icon a chart will automatically be created.

- **Excel 2003**. Right click in the pivot table / click the pivot chart icon.
  - Excel will create a chart on a new sheet.
- **Excel 2007**. Pivot Tools / Options / click the pivot chart icon.
  - Choose the type of chart you wish to see. Excel will create an embedded sheet.

Once the chart is created all the rules for charting seen earlier will apply. As it is a pivot chart you also get the option to move fields around as you wish or even include/exclude them.

Student Activity 48

This **Activity** is case-sensitive so make sure you use Upper and Lower case where indicated. Carry out the tasks in Column Order.

Column 1		Column 2	
Activity	Tick	**Activity**	Tick
Open the **ResultsPivotData** Workbook again from Engage		**Create** a Pivot Chart **Make the** chart type **Bar** **Locate** the chart in the pivot table worksheet	
Go to DataSheet and **highlight** Cells A1-E187		**Create titles** **Chart title** 'Exam Results 2010' **Value Axis** 'Percentage Score'	
Create a **Pivot Table** in a new worksheet		**Toggle** between the names and watch the chart change	
Page Field = Name **Row Field** = Result **Column Field** = Exam **Data Items** = **Max** of Score Format the result to %, 0 decimal places		**Save** the workbook as **Activity 48** in **Student Solutions**	

Find and replace

Introduction

This chapter will show you how to use a very useful function within Excel, 'find and replace'

KNOWLEDGE
2.2 Select and use a wide range of appropriate functions and formulas to meet calculation requirements.

Sometimes you discover that data has been input into a spreadsheet that you need to find or change. This is a fairly simple routine using the **Find and Replace** tool.

EXCEL 2000	EXCEL 2003	EXCEL 2007
/Edit/ /Find or Replace/	/Edit/ /Find or Replace/	/Home tab/ /Find & Select/ /Find or Replace

Shortcut
The simplest and fastest way to launch this tool is   **Ctrl+f**

When the tool is launched the following dialogue box appears:

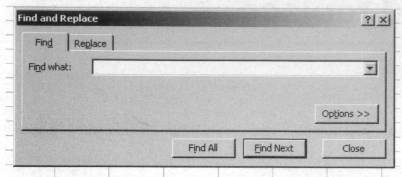

If you are trying to find a value you type it into the **Find what:** field. You can then choose to either find the next version of the value or find them all. If you opt to find them all Excel will present a list that you can scroll through.

There are also options that allow you to choose the case and position if you desire.

If your intention is to find and replace a value then you should select the **Replace** tab. You will then be faced with the following:

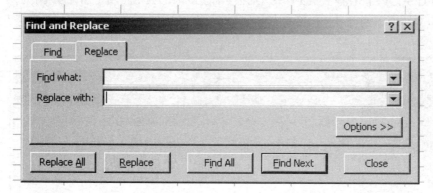

On this tab you again ask Excel to find the value and then type in a value to **Replace with**.

Student Activity 49

This **Activity** is case-sensitive so make sure you use Upper and Lower case where indicated. Carry out the tasks in Column Order.

Column 1		Column 2	
Activity	**Tick**	**Activity**	**Tick**
Open the **ResultsPivotData** Workbook from within Engage		**Replace all** and accept the result	
Find and Replace Ctrl+f **Find** Science and **Replace** it with Geology		**Find** all instances of Lowther and **replace** them with Luther	
		Save the workbook as **Activity 49** in **Student Solutions**	

'What-if' analysis

21

Introduction

This chapter will show you how to carry out the forecasting technique of 'what-if' analysis and also how to create named cell ranges.

> ### KNOWLEDGE
>
> 2.4 Select and use forecasting tools and techniques.

In this session you will be looking at different methods of **'What-If'** analysis. What-If analysis involves creating a spreadsheet and then asking the question "what if this/these figures were to change". There are a number of tools to look at:

- Creating **Manual** what-if solutions
- Data Tables
- Scenario Manager
- Goal Seek

21.1 Creating Manual 'What-If' solutions

In previous sessions you have created spreadsheets that used fixed cell references to get their data. These spreadsheets were manual 'what-if' solutions.

The overriding principle for 'what-if' solutions is do not 'hard code' variable data into formulas and functions. If you do this you will be unable to carry out 'what-if' without finding and replacing the hard coded data.

Student Activity 50

This **Activity** is case-sensitive so make sure you use Upper and Lower case where indicated. Carry out the tasks in Column Order.

Column 1		Column 2	
Activity	**Tick**	**Activity**	**Tick**
Open the **Activity 34** Workbook from the folder on your pc		**Go to** the **Pricing** worksheet and **unprotect** the sheet. [There is no password Change the value of **Supercruise** to £40000	
Note How the **Monthly Sales** worksheet relies on the data in the other 3 worksheets. Look in Cells D10-G13, to refresh your memory		**Return** to the **Monthly Sales** worksheet and note the new values in Cells D10-D13. **Return** to the **Pricing** worksheet and **Protect** it without a **Password**	
Note down the values in Cells D10-D13		**Save** the workbook as **Activity 50** in **Student Solutions**	

21.2   Data Tables

EXCEL 2000	EXCEL 2003	EXCEL 2007
/Data/ /Table/	/Data/ /Table/	/Data Tab/ /What-If Analysis/ /Data Table/

There are two types of **Data Tables**:

1. **Single Input:** This table allows you to create a spreadsheet with multiple formulas and functions to create a **solution**. The spreadsheet itself can have many variables and you can use a single input **Data Table** to evaluate a change in **one** of these variables – this is its draw back. However, there is nothing to stop you changing any of the other numbers once the table is formed.

2. **Two-Input:** This table works in the same way as above but in this instance you can create a table that allows a change to **two** variables – but only two.

Once your spreadsheet **solution** is created you will be ready create the **Data Table**. Activate the tool as above and you will be presented with the following dialogue box.

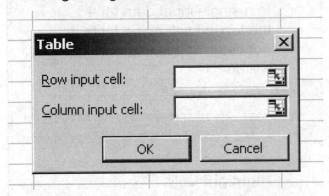

For a **single input** table you will need either a Row or Column input cell [not both. This is determined by the way in which the spreadsheet solution is constructed. [Either in a Row or a Column]. In a single input data table the top-left cell of the table is not used.

For **two Input** data tables you will need both Row and Column Inputs. In a two input data table the top-left is used to hold a formula that refers to the solution cell.

Student Activity 51

This **Activity** is case-sensitive so make sure you use Upper and Lower case where indicated. Carry out the tasks in Column Order.

Column 1		Column 2	
Activity	Tick	Activity	Tick
Open the **Data Table 1** Workbook from within Engage		**In** Cell I17 **create** a formula that takes the result of Cell D19	
Go to Cell D17 and **create** a Labour Cost total. **Multiply:** Production Volume × Hourly Rate × Labour Hours		**In** Cell J17 **create** a formula that takes the result of Cell D20	

Remember to ensure that the cell references are absolute		
Go to Cell D18 and **create** a Material Cost total. **Multiply:** Production Volume × Material Cost × Material Used **Remember** to ensure that the cell references are absolute	**Note** In a single input data table the top left cell of the table is not used. In this example this will be F17	
Go to Cell D19 and **create** a Fixed Cost total. **Accept** the figure in Cell D9 **Remember** to ensure that the cell references are absolute	**Highlight** Cells F17-J24	
Sum Cells D17-D19 **Copy** Cells C17-C20 **Go to** Cell G16 and **Paste Special and Transpose**	**Create** a Data Table, with **Column Input** , using Cell D7 as the input cell. This is the variable that we will examine	
In Cell F18 **type £10** increasing this by £1 in cells F19-F24	**Note** With this done you should have a table of data appear. It shows the outcomes if the material cost were to change from anywhere between £10 and£16	
In Cell G17 **create** a formula that takes the result of Cell D17	**Try** Changing other numbers in the range D4-D9 to see what happened to the content of your Data table	
In Cell H17 **create** a formula that takes the result of Cell D18	**Save** the workbook as **Activity 51** in **Student Solutions** on your pc	

KAPLAN PUBLISHING

Student Activity 52

This **Activity** is case-sensitive so make sure you use Upper and Lower case where indicated. Carry out the tasks in Column Order.

Column 1		Column 2	
Activity	**Tick**	**Activity**	**Tick**
Open the **Data Table 2** Workbook from within Engage			
In Cell D23, **create** a formula that multiplies Sales Volume × Sales Price		**Cells** G23 to G32 have been **pre-populated**	
In Cell D24, **create** a formula that multiplies Sales Volume × Hourly Rate × Labour Hours		In Cell G22 **create** a formula that refers to the **Net Profit cell** [D28]	
In Cell D25, **create** a formula that calculates total material cost. Sales Volume × material used × material cost per kg **If** the total material used [**sales volume × material used**] is **greater than** the Bulk Buy Quantity then the **material cost kg** is reduced by 4%, otherwise use the material cost per kg =IF((D4*$D$11)>=D13,((D4 *D10*D11)*(1-D12)),(D4*D10*D11))		**Highlight** cells G22-L32 **Insert** a **Data Table** The two variables that we are to compare are **sales volume** and **sales price** The **Row** input cell is sales price and the **Column** input cell is sales volume	
In Cell D26 **create** a formula that calculates **contribution**. Sales Revenue minus (total labour + total material cost)		**Custom Format** Cells H23-L32 as Currency, 0 decimal places and so that negative numbers are in red surrounded by **brackets**	

In Cell D27 **create** a formula that refers to the value in Cell D15		**Try** changing figures in the Row and Column input cells	
In Cell D28 **create** a formula that calculates **Net Profit**. Contribution minus Fixed Costs		**Try** changing figures in Cells D4 – D15, to see how sensitive the net profit is to change	
Cells H22 to L22 have been **pre-populated**		**Save** the workbook as **Activity 52** in **Student Solutions**	

21.3 Scenario Manager

Scenario manager is a tool that allows you to create scenarios of a particular solution. For example: you are trying to work out your product costs to calculate profits. However, you are uncertain as to the actual costs. Here, you could use **Scenario Manager** to create versions of the potential outcome. Once these have been created you can run a report to compare the potential results.

To activate scenario manager:

EXCEL 2000	EXCEL 2003	EXCEL 2007
/Tools/ /Scenarios/	/Tools/ /Scenarios/	/Data Tab/ /What-If Analysis/ /Scenario Manager/

When you are using **Scenario Manager** it will be very useful to **Name** some of the cells to make the reports more understandable. This technique can be used anywhere and anytime when you are creating spreadsheets, and so you should not consider that **naming** can only be used here. In fact naming cells and ranges makes the construction of formulas easier **and** makes them easier to understand.

Naming Cells and Ranges

Creating

To the left of the formula bar you will find a drop down box. This is known as the **Name Box**. This box shows the cell reference of the active cell.

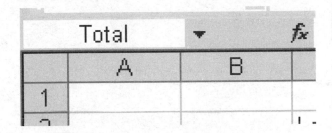

To create a named cell or range:

- Highlight the cell or cells you wish to name
- Click into the name box
- Type in the name you want.
  - The name you use must be a single word without spaces. You can use underscore as part of the name.

Editing/ deleting

If you need to edit a **Name** go to:

- **Excel 2003:** Insert / Name / Define.
- **Excel 2007:** Formulas tab / Name Manager

Highlight the name you wish to edit or delete and make your change.

Using Existing Titles

You may want to create names that are titles to rows or columns, and that already exist. Highlight the cell or range that you want and go to:

- **Excel 2003:** Insert / Name / Create
- **Excel 2007:** Formulas tab / Create from Selection

You will be given the following dialogue box:

You can then tell Excel where to find the names. The cells and names must be adjacent to each other.

Using names in formulas

To use a name in a formula you have two options.

1. Type in the **name**

2. Take the name from a list:

   a. **Excel 2003:** Insert / Name / Paste

   b. **Excel 2007:** Formulas tab / Use in Formula

 Student Activity 53

This **Activity** is case-sensitive so make sure you use Upper and Lower case where indicated. Carry out the tasks in Column Order.

Column 1		Column 2	
Activity	Tick	Activity	Tick
Open the **Cell Naming** Workbook **Highlight** Cells A1 – B2 **Insert** / Name / Create [Excel 2003] **Formulas** / Create from selection [Excel 2007] Accept the solution offered		In Cell D19 type =sum(January) In E,F and G19 **create** a sum formula using the correct range name for the column. **Note** you cannot drag the formula to the right.	
		In Cell B26 **create** a Name for the cell called Sales_Revenue	

Highlight Cells D6 – G17 Create a name as above Accept the solution offered	Save the workbook as Activity 53 in Student Solutions	163

Dealing with Scenario Manager

The tool when activated needs to know which cells will be used as the **changing cells**. These cells will be altered by scenario manager once you have created your scenarios and run your report. You will also need to create a name for the scenario.

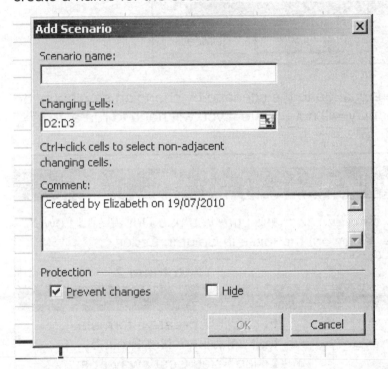

When you **Add** the scenario to the manager you will be asked for values for the **changing cells**.

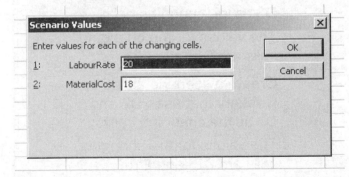

The tool will also need to know which cells you will be using for your results. For example you may be using cells to calculate profit and these you would need to tell scenario manager. Scenario Manager will ask for the results cells when you run the Summary Report.

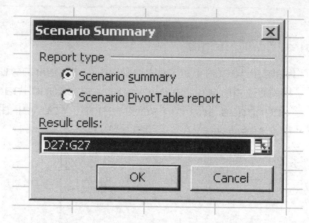

Note: that if you make a change to the scenario by changing say, hours or material used the Summary will not update – you will need to run a new summary.

Student Activity 54

This **Activity** is case-sensitive so make sure you use Upper and Lower case where indicated. Carry out the tasks in Column Order.

Column 1		Column 2	
Activity	**Tick**	**Activity**	**Tick**
Open the **Scenario Manager** workbook from Engage		**In** cell D27 **create** a formula that calculates Net Profit by taking Fixed Cost away from Total Contribution	
In Cell D2, **insert** a name for the cell LabourRate		**Create** a scenario called **Preferred** that uses D2 and D3 as the changing cells. The values for the changing cells are £14 and £16	
In Cell D3, **insert** a name for the cell MaterialCost		**Create** a scenario called **Unlikely** that uses D2 and D3 as the changing cells. The values for the changing cells are £13 and £15	

In Cell D12 **create** a formula for Labour cost per unit LabourRate × Hours in Production Copy the formula to cells E12 and F12		**Create** a scenario called **Moderate Change** that uses D2 and D3 as the changing cells. The values for the changing cells are £16and £18	
In Cell D13 **create** a formula for Material cost per unit MaterialCost × Material Quantity per Unit Copy the formula to cells E13 and F13		**Create** a scenario called **Extreme** that uses D2 and D3 as the changing cells. The values for the changing cells are £20 and £18	
In cell D18 **create** a formula that calculates Selling Price minus Total Variable Costs Copy the formula to E18 and F18		**Create** a Scenario Summary Report that uses Cells D27 – G27 as the Results Cells	
In cell D22 **create** a formula that multiplies Contribution per Unit by Sales Volume		**View** the results.	
In cell D27, **insert** a name for the cell Alpha_Net_Profit Do the same for Bravo and Charlie in cells E27 and F27		**Save** the workbook as **Activity 54** in **Student Solutions**	

21.4 Goal Seek

Goal Seek is 'what-if' in reverse. Here a tool is used to determine a change to a variable that will result in the solution that you want.

EXCEL 2000	EXCEL 2003	EXCEL 2007
/Tools/ /Goal Seek/	/Tools/ /Goal Seek/	/Data Tab/ /What-If Analysis/ /Goal Seek/

For example you may want to make a Net Profit of £10,000 but are unsure of how much a variable such as labour rate will have to change to create this profit.

When you launch Goal Seek you are faced with the following dialogue box:

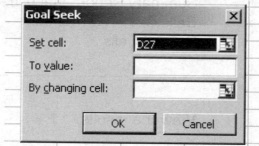

You are asked:

* To **set** a particular cell
* To a particular **value**
* By **changing** a particular cell

Student Activity 55

This **Activity** is case-sensitive so make sure you use Upper and Lower case where indicated. Carry out the tasks in Column Order.

Column 1		Column 2	
Activity	**Tick**	**Activity**	**Tick**
Open the **Goal Seek** workbook from Engage		**Highlight** cell E27 Launch Goal Seek **Set** Cell E27 to £15000 By **changing** cell D3	
Highlight cell D27 Launch Goal Seek		**Note** the changes	
Set Cell D27 to £12000 By **changing** cell D2		**Save** the workbook as **Activity 55** in **Student Solutions**	

Sometimes a solution cannot be found. If this is the case you will need to adjust the values you are asking Goal Seek to find till you get a correct answer.

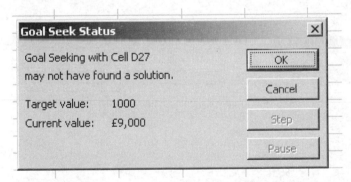

Don't forget to check that the variable is actually involved in the calculation.

Student Activity 56

This **Activity** is case-sensitive so make sure you use Upper and Lower case where indicated. Carry out the tasks in Column Order.

Column 1		Column 2	
Activity	**Tick**	**Activity**	**Tick**
Open the **Goal Seek** Workbook from Engage		Make the solution fit the columns	
Highlight cell D27 Launch Goal Seek		**Note** the changes and what happens with Goal Seek	
Set Cell D27 to £1000 By **changing** cell D3		**Save** the workbook as **Activity 56** in **Student Solutions**	

Analysis tools

Introduction

This chapter will show you how launch an 'add-in' and to understand how to use analysis tools.

KNOWLEDGE
2.3 Select and use a range of tools and techniques to analyse and interpret data to meet requirements.
3.7 Use auditing tools to identify and respond appropriately to any problems with spreadsheets.

Within Excel there is a selection of **Analysis Tools** that you need to be aware of. These tools do not come as standard on any menu and to use them you will need to activate an **Add-In**

EXCEL 2000	EXCEL 2003	EXCEL 2007
/Tools/	/Tools/	/Excel Icon/
/Add Ins/	/Add Ins/	/Excel Options/
/Analysis ToolPak/	/Analysis ToolPak/	/Add-Ins/
		/Manage: Excel Add ins/
		/Go/
		/Analysis ToolPak/

The **Analysis Tools** that you need to be aware of are:

1. Histogram

2. Moving Average

3. Random Number

4. Rank & Percentile

5. Sampling

Once the tools have been installed they can be accessed via:

EXCEL 2000	EXCEL 2003	EXCEL 2007
/Tools/ /Data Analysis/ /Select Tool/	/Tools/ /Data Analysis/ /Select Tool/	/Data Tab/ /Data Analysis/ /Select Tool/

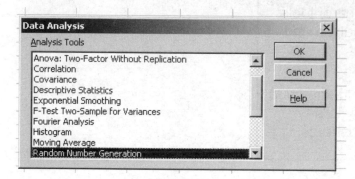

22.1 Histogram

The purpose of a Histogram is to graphically illustrate and summarise the distribution of a univariate data set. A univariate data set would be a single set of data such as a range of ages.

When the tool is launched you are presented with the following dialogue box:

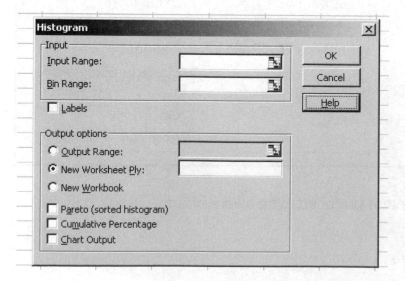

Things that you need to consider:

- **Input Range:** This is the data that you wish to include in the **histogram**

- **Bin Range:** In a histogram you can select a number of ranges or **bins** that you wish to group the data in. If you do not create and select **bins** then Excel will create 10 bins for you based on an equal distribution of the data in the **input range**.

- **Labels:** Excel will create suitable labels for the histogram, however, you should tick this box if the 1st row or column of your data contains labels

- **Output Range:** Select the cell where you would like the output table to be.

- **New Worksheet Ply:** If you wish for the output table to be in a new worksheet select it here.

- **New Workbook:** If you wish for the output to be in a new workbook, select this option.

- **Pareto (sorted histogram):** Select to present data in the output table in descending order of frequency. If this check box is cleared, Excel presents the data in ascending order and omits the three rightmost columns that contain the sorted data.

- **Cumulative Percentage:** Select this if you want Excel to create a cumulative percentage column in the output table. Excel will also create a cumulative percentage line on the histogram chart.

- **Chart Output:** Select this if you wish Excel to create a chart. Excel will create an embedded chart. Once the chart has been created all the charting options seen earlier are available

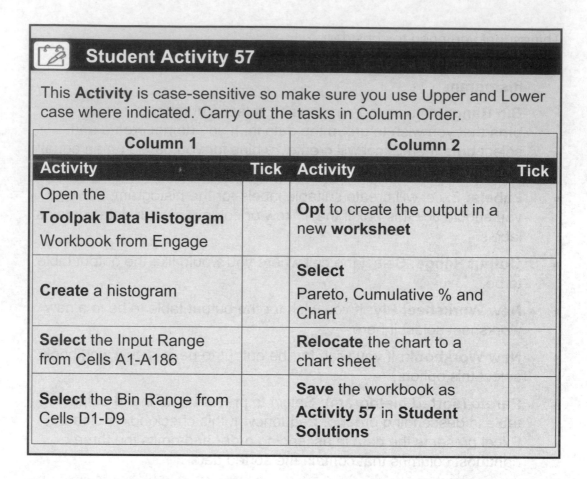

Student Activity 57

This **Activity** is case-sensitive so make sure you use Upper and Lower case where indicated. Carry out the tasks in Column Order.

Column 1		Column 2	
Activity	Tick	Activity	Tick
Open the **Toolpak Data Histogram** Workbook from Engage		**Opt** to create the output in a new **worksheet**	
Create a histogram		**Select** Pareto, Cumulative % and Chart	
Select the Input Range from Cells A1-A186		**Relocate** the chart to a chart sheet	
Select the Bin Range from Cells D1-D9		**Save** the workbook as **Activity 57** in **Student Solutions**	

22.2 Moving average

A **moving average** is used by accountants to smooth out fluctuations in numerical data in a Time-Series, in order that trends in the data can be found. Moving averages will form part of your studies. It is possible to create your own moving average, but Excel provides a tool to do this for you.

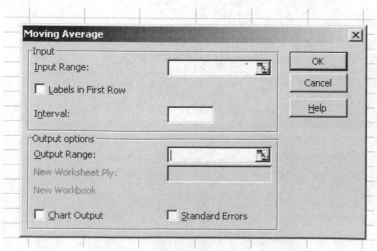

Things that you need to consider:

- **Input Range:** This is the data that you wish to include in the **moving average**.

- **Labels:** Excel will create suitable labels for the moving average, however, you should tick this box if the 1st row of your data contains labels

- **Interval:** This refers to the grouping of the data. For example you might be grouping your data into quarters of a year, and therefore your interval would be four. The default **interval** is three.

- **Output Range:** Select the cell where you would like the output table to be. There is no option to put the output in a new workbook or worksheet.

- **Chart Output:** Select this if you wish Excel to create a chart. Excel will create an embedded chart. Once the chart has been created all the charting options seen earlier are available.

- **Standard Error:** Select this only if you want Excel to add a column of data showing the standard error.
    - The **standard error** is a method of measurement of how far the values in the input range are from an average calculation. Not covered in this syllabus

Student Activity 58

This **Activity** is case-sensitive so make sure you use Upper and Lower case where indicated. Carry out the tasks in Column Order.

Column 1		Column 2	
Activity	**Tick**	**Activity**	**Tick**
Open the **Toolpak Data Moving Average** Workbook from Engage		**Opt** to create the output starting in Cell E1	
Create a moving average		**Create** a chart	
Select the Input Range from Cells B1-B24.		**Relocate** the chart to a **chart-sheet**	
Labels in 1st Row			
Interval is 4		**Save** the workbook as **Activity 58** in **Student Solutions**	

22.3   Random Numbers

Random numbers are commonly used in sampling methods. Sampling is covered as part of your syllabus. The tool that Excel provides is complex and therefore only one form of **random number** generator will be used for the sake of simplicity. You will only be looking at a random number generator that uses **uniform** distribution

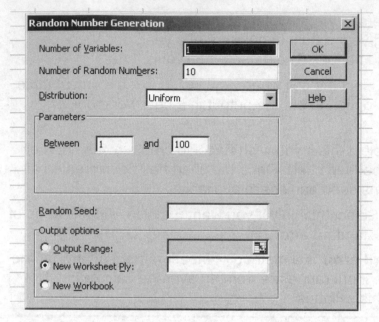

- **Number of Variables:** Enter here how many columns of **random numbers** you require.

- **Number of Random Numbers:** Enter here how many random numbers you require in each column.

- **Distribution:** This is the complex area of this tool. Different types of **distribution** are used for different purposes – these are outside of the syllabus. We will only be looking at a **uniform** distribution.

- **Parameters:** Enter here a range between which you want the numbers generated

- **Random Seed:** A value can be entered from which the random numbers will be generated. This can be used to ensure that the same numbers are generated in the future.

- **Output Options:** These you have seen before.

Student Activity 59

This **Activity** is case-sensitive so make sure you use Upper and Lower case where indicated. Carry out the tasks in Column Order.

Column 1		Column 2	
Activity	**Tick**	**Activity**	**Tick**
Open a **New** workbook		**Set** the **parameters** between 1 and 100 **Do NOT** enter a number for a **Random Seed**	
Create a random number generator		**Output** to a new worksheet	
Select the number of variables as 2		**Note** the output. **Round** the output to 0 decimal places and **paste-special** values	
Select the number of **random numbers** as 10		**Delete** the ROUND functions	
Select Uniform Distribution		**Save** the workbook as **Activity 59** in **Student Solutions**	

22.4   Rank and Percentile

The Rank and Percentile tool produces a four column table that contains the **ordinal** and **percentile** rank of each value in a data set.

- **Ordinal:** A number that defines a things position in a data set

- **Percentile:** Here you get a percentage score for a number and all numbers below it in your data set.

The four columns represent:

1. Whereabouts in the data-set the value comes from.

2. The value of the number

3. Its Rank – those values that are the same have the same rank

4. Its percentile score – the percentage of numbers in the data-set that are the same or below it

When you launch the tool you are faced with the following dialogue box.

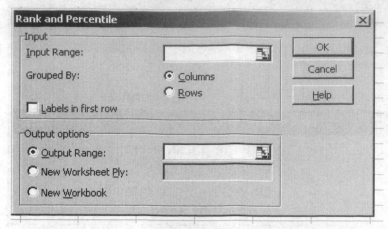

- **Input Range:** The items that you wish to rank.

- **Grouped By:** Choose whether the data is in columns or rows and whether there are **labels.**

- **Output options:** These you have seen before.

Student Activity 60

This **Activity** is case-sensitive so make sure you use Upper and Lower case where indicated. Carry out the tasks in Column Order.

Column 1		Column 2	
Activity	**Tick**	**Activity**	**Tick**
Open the **Toolpak Data Rank and Percentile** Workbook from Engage		**Output** to a new worksheet	
Create using the Rank and Percentile tool		**Note** rows 7 and 8	
The **input range** is Cells A1 – A186			
NO labels		**Save** the workbook as **Activity 60** in **Student Solutions**	

22.5   Sampling

Sampling is part of your syllabus. The sampling tool creates a sample from a population by using the input range as the population. When the tool is launched you are faced with the following dialogue box:

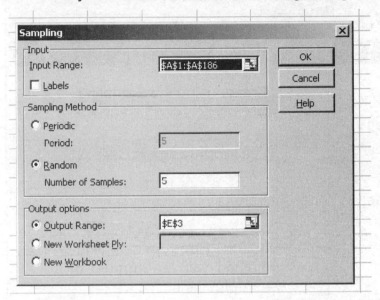

- **Input Range:** The items in your population that you wish to pick your sample from.

- **Labels:** this has been covered above.

- **Sampling method:**

  - **Periodic:** This is where you choose to select every nth value in your population. For example every 9th value.

  - **Random:** This is where we allow Excel to choose our sample at random from the population.

- **Number of samples:** How many items do you wish to choose from the population.

Activity 2

This **Activity** is case-sensitive so make sure you use Upper and Lower case where indicated. Carry out the tasks in Column Order.

Column 1		Column 2	
Activity	**Tick**	**Activity**	**Tick**
Open the **Toolpak Data Sampling** Workbook from Engage		**Create** using the Sampling tool	
Create using the Sampling tool		The **input range** is Cells A1 – A100	
The **input range** is Cells A1 – A100		**NO** labels	
NO labels		**Use** the **Random** sampling method, with the **number of samples** being 10	
Use the periodic sampling method with a **period** of 5		**Output** to a new worksheet **Re-label** the worksheet as **Random**	
Output to a new worksheet **Re-label** the worksheet as **Periodic**		**Note** the output in **both** worksheets	
		Save the workbook as **Activity 61** in **Student Solutions**	

INDEX

KAPLAN PUBLISHING